Also in This Series

Family Favorite Casserole Recipes:
103 Comforting Breakfast Casseroles, Dinner Ideas,
and Desserts Everyone Will Love

No-Bake Desserts:
103 Easy Recipes for No-Bake Cookies, Bars, and Treats

Everyday Dinner Ideas:
103 Easy Recipes for Chicken, Pasta, and
Other Dishes Everyone Will Love

Easy Cookie Recipes:
103 Best Recipes for Chocolate Chip Cookies, Cake Mix Creations,
Bars, and Holiday Treats Everyone Will Love

Retro Recipes from the '50s and '60s:
103 Vintage Appetizers, Dinners, and Drinks Everyone Will Love

Essential Slow Cooker Recipes:
103 Fuss-Free Slow Cooker Meals Everyone Will Love

Easy Chicken Recipes:
103 Inventive Soups, Salads, Casseroles, and
Dinners Everyone Will Love

Homemade Soup Recipes

103 Easy Recipes for Soups, Stews, Chilis, and Chowders Everyone Will Love

Addie Gundry

St. Martin's Griffin ⚞ New York

HOMEMADE SOUP RECIPES. Text and photography © 2018 by Prime Publishing LLC. All rights reserved. Printed in the United States of America. For information, address St. Martin's Press, 175 Fifth Avenue, New York, N.Y. 10010.

www.stmartins.com

Photography by Megan Von Schönhoff and Tom Krawczyk

The Library of Congress Cataloging-in-Publication Data is available upon request.

ISBN 978-1-250-16172-7 (paperback)
ISBN 978-1-250-16171-0 (ebook)

Our books may be purchased in bulk for promotional, educational, or business use. Please contact your local bookseller or the Macmillan Corporate and Premium Sales Department at 1-800-221-7945, extension 5442, or by email at MacmillanSpecialMarkets@macmillan.com.

First Edition: March 2018

10 9 8 7 6 5 4 3 2 1

Homemade Soup
Recipes

To Jessica, my editor and friend.
Thank you for your attention to detail,
continuous patience, and love for the job.
You make these books better
with every part you touch.

Contents

4
Vegetarian Soups

Introduction

The first thing I think of when I imagine soup is wanting nothing more than to shut myself inside and stay in my pajamas on a cold, dreary, rainy day. I think of days home from school watching daytime TV in between naps, sipping soup like a magic potion, willing my body back to health.

While soup has been a comfort during times when I've felt blue, I also can't help but think of times when soup has brought me joy. I picture my friends chowing down on a bowl of Country Chicken Stew (page 159) before heading out for a second wave of trick-or-treating, and the Extra Creamy Mushroom Soup (page 135) that was served as the first course at my wedding rehearsal dinner. I remember cooking a huge batch of Classic Slow Cooker Chili (page 184) to devour while watching football with my husband and our friends, and enjoying Cold Cucumber Soup (page 5) while the sun still shone in the distance on a lazy summer night.

The appeal of soup isn't its temperature; it's about the flavor. It's about the combination of spicy and sour you get from Mexican Chicken Lime Soup (page 83), the coziness of a cheesy Beefy Nacho Soup (page 67), and the sweet, creamy goodness of Butternut Squash Soup (page 32). It's about the way the spices mix with the meat and veggies to create a delightful, simmering, flavorful dish that can be dressed up or down, depending on the occasion.

Why 103? When you come to our house, we want you to know you can always bring a friend . . . or two, or three. One hundred felt so rigid, and whether I'm cheering up someone who's blue or enjoying a lunch in with friends, there is always room for three more. I hope that this book, filled with soups you can enjoy all year long, will bring comfort and joy to your home.

—Addie Gundry

1

Chilled Soups

Soup truly is a year-round dish. While I stock up on heartier, meatier stews in the dead of winter, my summers are full of chilled soups, from sweet veggie gazpachos to colorful fruit soups. And when I'm expecting company and want to present a sophisticated and impressive starter, I can always rely on chilled soups to start a meal off right.

Cold Cucumber Soup

Yield: Serves 1–2 | Prep Time: 5 minutes | Chill Time: 4 hours

Yogurt mixed with cucumber creates a sweet, silky texture that's so refreshing at the end of a long day. The hint of lemon zest really makes this particular recipe shine, giving it a welcome burst of bright citrus flavor.

INGREDIENTS

1 cup diced peeled English cucumber

½ cup vegetable broth

1 cup plain Greek yogurt

1 teaspoon Dijon mustard

1 tablespoon minced shallot

1 garlic clove, minced

2 tablespoons fresh dill, plus chopped dill for garnish

2 tablespoons fresh parsley

1 teaspoon herbes de Provence

1 teaspoon lemon zest

1 teaspoon fresh lemon juice

Crème fraîche, for garnish

DIRECTIONS

1. In a food processor, combine the cucumber, broth, yogurt, mustard, shallot, garlic, dill, parsley, herbes de Provence, lemon zest, and lemon juice. Process until smooth. Transfer to an airtight container and chill for 4 hours or up to 4 days.

2. Pour the chilled soup into bowls. Garnish with a dollop of crème fraîche and chopped fresh dill and serve.

Sweet Corn Gazpacho

Yield: Serves 4 | Prep Time: 15 minutes plus 30 minutes resting time | Cook Time: N/A

Growing up in Minnesota, I was always looking for new ways to cook with the abundance of corn I saw all around me. This Sweet Corn Gazpacho is perfect because it's creamy while being totally dairy-free.

INGREDIENTS

2 pounds yellow tomatoes, chopped

2 yellow bell peppers, seeded and chopped

Kernels from 3 ears corn

¼ cup chopped shallots

2 garlic cloves, chopped

¼ jalapeño, seeded and chopped

2 teaspoons sea salt, plus more as needed

½ cup olive oil, plus more for garnish

¼ cup white balsamic vinegar

1 teaspoon lime zest

2 tablespoons fresh lime juice

Chopped fresh chives, for garnish

DIRECTIONS

1. In a large bowl, combine the tomatoes, bell peppers, corn kernels, shallots, garlic, and jalapeño. Sprinkle with the sea salt and let stand for 30 minutes.

2. Pour the corn mixture into a blender or food processor and add the olive oil. Blend the soup until smooth or, if you prefer, leave a bit chunky.

3. Add the vinegar, lime zest, and lime juice. Taste and season with more salt as needed.

4. Serve at room temperature or chilled, garnished with a drizzle of olive oil and some chives.

Strawberry-Orange Soup

Yield: Serves 6 | Prep Time: 10 minutes | Chill Time: 1 hour

When my girlfriends came over for a spa day, I served this Strawberry-Orange Soup. I just love the bright pink coloring, and the fruit combined with a minty touch left us all feeling wonderfully relaxed and rejuvenated.

INGREDIENTS

4 cups fresh strawberries, hulled

½ cup confectioners' sugar

1 cup fresh orange juice

Juice of ½ lime

3 tablespoons chopped fresh mint leaves, plus 6 fresh mint leaves, chopped, for garnish

1 tablespoon orange zest

1 teaspoon granulated sugar

1 tablespoon slivered almonds

¼ cup crème fraîche

DIRECTIONS

1. In a food processor, puree the strawberries until smooth. Add the confectioners' sugar and puree for 1 minute. Add the orange juice and lime juice and puree for 1 minute more.

2. Add 1 tablespoon of the mint and process for another minute. Transfer to an airtight container and refrigerate for 1 hour.

3. In a small bowl, combine the remaining 2 tablespoons mint, the orange zest, granulated sugar, and almonds. Add the crème fraîche and mix well.

4. Ladle the chilled soup into bowls or mason jars for serving. Top the soup with a dollop of the crème fraîche mixture and mint leaves.

Pea and Mint Soup

Yield: Serves 4 | Prep Time: 5 minutes | Cook Time: 20 minutes

When I'm serving a fancy, multicourse dinner, I like to serve a palate-cleansing soup in between big courses, and this Pea and Mint Soup is one of my go-to favorites. If you grow your own mint, now's the time for it to shine!

INGREDIENTS

1 tablespoon unsalted butter

1 large leek, white and light green parts only, chopped and rinsed well

2 cups chicken broth

2 tablespoons fresh lemon juice

2 sprigs fresh mint

1 teaspoon chopped fresh chives

1 pound frozen baby peas

Sea salt and freshly ground black pepper

¼ cup crème fraîche, for garnish

1 tablespoon heavy cream, for garnish

Chopped fresh chives, for garnish

DIRECTIONS

1. In a medium pot, melt the butter over medium-high heat. Add the leek and cook for 1 to 2 minutes.

2. Add the broth, lemon juice, mint sprigs, and chives. Bring to a boil.

3. Add the peas, return to a boil, reduce the heat to medium-low, and simmer for 5 minutes.

4. Turn off the heat and let the soup cool for 5 to 10 minutes.

5. Remove the mint sprigs with a slotted spoon. Transfer the soup to a blender or blend directly in the pot using an immersion blender and puree until smooth.

6. Season with salt and pepper. The soup can be served hot or cold. If serving cold, cover and refrigerate for 1 hour.

7. Ladle the soup into bowls. Mix the crème fraîche with the cream, then dollop it on top of the soup, swirl it around, and top it with some chives.

Spanish Gazpacho

Yield: Serves 6 | Prep Time: 15 minutes | Chill Time: 1 hour

One memorable evening while I was studying abroad in Europe, Spanish Gazpacho came to my rescue. My roommates and I had been living on microwaveable food and takeout, due to the sweltering heat (and our lack of air-conditioning), and we needed to find something, anything, that was full of veggies and nutrients. Not only did this hit the spot, but we wound up making it twice more that month!

INGREDIENTS

2 pounds vine-ripe tomatoes, chopped

2 garlic cloves, minced

½ English cucumber, peeled and chopped, plus extra for garnish

1 yellow or orange bell pepper, seeded and chopped

½ cup chopped shallots, plus more for garnish

¼ cup sherry vinegar or red wine vinegar

1 tablespoon balsamic vinegar

¾ cup olive oil, plus more for garnish

½ teaspoon ground cumin

¼ teaspoon smoked paprika

¼ teaspoon cayenne pepper

Sea salt

Chunk of French or ciabatta bread (about 4 inches), cut into 1-inch pieces

Diced cucumber, for garnish

DIRECTIONS

1. In a blender, combine the tomatoes, garlic, cucumber, bell pepper, and shallots. Start to pulse, then slowly add the sherry vinegar, balsamic vinegar, and olive oil. Blend until smooth.

2. Add the cumin, paprika, and cayenne. Taste and season with salt.

3. Add the bread and pulse until blended in.

4. Transfer the soup to an airtight container and refrigerate for 1 hour or longer.

5. Pour the soup into bowls. Garnish with some chopped cucumber, shallots, and a drizzle of olive oil.

Cantaloupe Soup

Yield: Serves 4 | Prep Time: 10 minutes | Chill Time: 2 hours

I call this my "dessert soup" because it's just so sweet! I try to have something a little healthier than ice cream on hand throughout the summer when my friends bring their kids over, and cantaloupe is chock-full of vitamins A and C.

INGREDIENTS

1 cantaloupe, peeled, seeded, and cut into 1-inch chunks

⅓ cup crème fraîche

1 tablespoon grated fresh ginger

1 teaspoon honey

¼ teaspoon ground nutmeg

1 teaspoon fresh lime juice

Pinch of sea salt

Fresh mint leaves, for garnish

DIRECTIONS

1. In a food processor, puree the cantaloupe (reserving some for garnish, if desired), crème fraîche, ginger, honey, nutmeg, lime juice, and salt until smooth.

2. Transfer the soup to an airtight container and refrigerate for 2 hours or longer.

3. Pour the soup into bowls. Garnish with extra cantaloupe chunks, if desired, and fresh mint leaves.

NOTE

Add additional honey if you want the soup to be a bit sweeter.

2

Slow Cooker Soups

Soups and slow cookers go hand in hand. Allowing the broth, meat, and spices to slowly simmer all day gives the ingredients plenty of time to marinate and combine in the most enticing ways. You achieve a rich flavor without needing to stand over a hot stovetop, but the finished product can still warm you up when there's a chill in the air. The Italian Wedding Soup (page 20) tastes even better when the ingredients have time to "marry," while the Steak and Potato Soup (page 31) cooks the beef to perfection throughout the day.

Kielbasa Soup

Yield: Serves 8 | Prep Time: 15 minutes | Cook Time: 4–5 hours on High or 8–10 hours on Low

Kielbasa is a signature ingredient in many German, Polish, and Ukrainian dishes, and I love how the heartiness of the meat interacts with the various veggies in this slow-cooker supper. There's very little prep work that needs to be done, making this a great dish to start in the morning before you go to work, so you come home to a fully cooked dinner.

INGREDIENTS

1 (16-ounce) bag dried brown lentils, rinsed and drained

10 cups beef broth

1 (14-ounce) can fire-roasted diced tomatoes

½–¾ pound carrots, grated

2 celery stalks, chopped

2 tablespoons minced garlic

1 teaspoon Worcestershire sauce

¼ teaspoon hot sauce

1 bay leaf

½ cup fresh parsley, chopped

½ teaspoon garlic powder

½ teaspoon freshly ground black pepper, plus more as needed

¼ teaspoon ground nutmeg

2 cups cubed kielbasa

1 tablespoon red wine vinegar

Kosher salt (optional)

DIRECTIONS

1. In a 6-quart slow cooker, combine the lentils, broth, tomatoes, carrots, celery, garlic, Worcestershire sauce, hot sauce, bay leaf, parsley, garlic powder, pepper, and nutmeg. Stir to combine.

2. Add the kielbasa and mix.

3. Cover and cook for 4 to 5 hours on High or 8 to 10 hours on Low, until the lentils are cooked.

4. Add the vinegar. Taste and season with salt and pepper, if desired. Remove the bay leaf, ladle into bowls, and serve.

Italian Wedding Soup

Yield: Serves 4–6 | Prep Time: 15 minutes | Cook Time: 6–8 hours on Low

The name Italian Wedding Soup comes from the Italian phrase *minestra maritata*, which means "married soup." Now, that doesn't mean it's typically made for someone's upcoming nuptials; instead, it refers to the marriage of flavors between the greens and the broth.

INGREDIENTS

8 cups chicken broth

3 carrots, chopped

½ onion, diced

1 tablespoon dried parsley

1 teaspoon dried oregano

2 garlic cloves, finely minced

Kosher salt and freshly ground black pepper

1½ pounds prepared frozen turkey meatballs

1 pound baby spinach

1 cup uncooked pastina or other small pasta

Crusty bread, for serving

DIRECTIONS

1. In a 6-quart slow cooker, combine the broth, carrots, onion, parsley, oregano, and garlic. Season with salt and pepper. Cover and cook on Low for 6 hours.

2. One hour before serving, taste and adjust the seasoning, if needed. Add the frozen meatballs. Cover and continue to cook.

3. Twenty minutes before serving, stir in the baby spinach and pastina. Cover once more and cook until the pasta is al dente.

4. Serve in large bowls with crusty bread.

Chicken Potpie Soup

Yield: Serves 6 | Prep Time: 20 minutes | Cook Time: 4 hours on High or 8 hours on Low

It's hard to beat chicken potpie for dinner. In this soup, the creamy broth and steaming vegetables are like a warm, cozy hug protecting you from any unsavory weather outside. The biscuits take the place of a buttery crust, making this slow cooker soup a unique version of a retro family favorite.

INGREDIENTS

1 pound boneless, skinless chicken breasts, cut into bite-size pieces

1 small onion, diced

3 celery stalks, diced

2 garlic cloves, minced

2 carrots, diced

1 cup frozen corn kernels

1 cup frozen peas

1 pound potatoes, peeled and diced

2 (10.5-ounce) cans condensed cream of chicken soup

1 cup half-and-half

1½–2 teaspoons herbes de Provence

½ teaspoon kosher salt

½ teaspoon freshly ground black pepper

2 bay leaves

1 (16.3-ounce) can refrigerated biscuits

DIRECTIONS

1. Place the chicken in a 6-quart slow cooker. Add the onion, celery, garlic, carrots, corn, peas, and potatoes. Mix together.

2. In a small bowl, combine the chicken soup, half-and-half, herbes de Provence, salt, and pepper. Pour over the chicken and vegetables. Add the bay leaves.

3. Cover and cook on High for 4 hours or on Low for 8 hours.

4. About 30 minutes before the end of cooking, bake the biscuits according to the package directions.

5. Remove the bay leaves. Ladle the soup into bowls and serve with biscuits.

Zuppa Toscana

Yield: Serves 8 | Prep Time: 10 minutes | Cook Time: 4–5 hours on Low or 2 hours on High

The best part about this soup is how incredibly creamy it is. I use 2% milk to make it a bit lighter, but if you want something richer, feel free to use whole milk instead. I also recommend using hot sausage over mild, just to give the dish a kick.

INGREDIENTS

1 pound hot or mild bulk Italian sausage

Kosher salt and freshly ground black pepper

1 small onion, finely diced

½ teaspoon minced garlic

4 cups low-sodium chicken broth

1 pound baby yellow potatoes, quartered

¼ cup all-purpose flour

2 cups 2% milk

2 cups chopped baby spinach

DIRECTIONS

1. In a large pot, brown the sausage over medium-high heat until no longer pink and season with salt and pepper. Drain the excess fat from the pot.

2. Put the sausage, onion, garlic, broth, and potatoes in a 6-quart slow cooker. Cover and cook on Low for 4 to 5 hours, or on High for 2 hours.

3. About 45 minutes before serving, combine the flour and milk with a whisk until smooth. Stir into the soup. Cover and continue cooking until the potatoes are cooked and the soup has thickened slightly.

4. About 5 minutes before serving, turn the slow cooker off and stir in the spinach. Let the spinach wilt slightly.

5. Taste and adjust the seasoning as needed. Ladle into bowls and serve.

Sausage Lentil Soup

Yield: Serves 4–6 | Prep Time: 15 minutes | Cook Time: 4–5 hours on High or 8–10 hours on Low

This dish uses one of my favorite soup tricks. Because the soup is simmered for so long in the slow cooker, there's no need to remove the thyme leaves from the stems. By leaving them on, you can still enjoy the flavor in the soup without spending all that time removing the leaves.

INGREDIENTS

5 cups beef broth

1 cup red wine

1 pound smoked sausage, cut crosswise into ¼-inch-thick slices

1 (16-ounce) bag dried brown lentils, rinsed and drained

1 cup sliced carrots

5–6 thyme sprigs

1 small onion, diced

2 garlic cloves, crushed

1 bay leaf

6 whole black peppercorns

1 teaspoon kosher salt

1 tablespoon Worcestershire sauce

DIRECTIONS

1. In a 6-quart slow cooker, combine the broth, wine, sausage, lentils, carrots, thyme, onion, garlic, bay leaf, peppercorns, salt, and Worcestershire sauce. Stir to combine.

2. Cover and cook on High for 4 to 5 hours, until the lentils are tender.

3. Remove the bay leaf and thyme stems, ladle into bowls, and serve.

Corned Beef and Cabbage Soup

Yield: Serves 6–8 | Prep Time: 20 minutes | Cook Time: 3–4 hours on High or 7–8 hours on Low

My favorite part about this recipe is the addition of a bottle of beer. Beer adds a rich, earthy flavor to the soup, lending much more depth to the dish.

INGREDIENTS

1½ pounds corned beef, cut into bite-size chunks

1½ pounds baby red potatoes, halved

2 carrots, diced

2 celery stalks, diced

1 onion, diced

2 garlic cloves, minced

1 small head cabbage, cored and shredded

1 bay leaf

4 cups chicken broth

1 (12-ounce) bottle beer (any kind, but I recommend a pale ale)

¼ teaspoon dry mustard

½ teaspoon smoked paprika

½ teaspoon kosher salt, plus more as needed

½ teaspoon freshly ground black pepper, plus more as needed

DIRECTIONS

1. In a 6-quart slow cooker, combine the corned beef, potatoes, carrots, celery, onion, garlic, cabbage, bay leaf, broth, beer, mustard, paprika, salt, and pepper. Toss to combine.

2. Cover and cook on High for 3 to 4 hours or on Low for 7 to 8 hours, until the corned beef and vegetables are tender.

3. Remove the bay leaf. Season with additional salt and pepper, if needed. Ladle into bowls and serve.

Steak and Potato Soup

Yield: Serves 6–8 | Prep Time: 15 minutes | Cook Time: 4–5 hours on High or 8–10 hours on Low

The red pepper flakes, chili, and cayenne pepper add a bit of a kick to this essential "I'm holing myself up in my house all day and watching movies under a blanket" soup. The thick, juicy chunks of beef pair well with the chunky, hearty potato pieces for a feel-good dish.

INGREDIENTS

1½ pounds chuck roast, cut into 1-inch chunks

½ cup chopped onion

3 garlic cloves, minced

3 cups cubed Yukon Gold potatoes

1 (14-ounce) can fire-roasted diced tomatoes

1 (6-ounce) can tomato paste

4 cups beef broth

1 tablespoon Worcestershire sauce

1 tablespoon chili powder

1 teaspoon ground cumin

½ teaspoon cayenne pepper

½ teaspoon smoked paprika

¼ teaspoon red pepper flakes

½ teaspoon kosher salt

¼ teaspoon freshly ground black pepper

Chopped green onions, for garnish

DIRECTIONS

1. In a 6-quart slow cooker, combine the chuck roast, onion, garlic, potatoes, tomatoes, tomato paste, broth, Worcestershire sauce, chili powder, cumin, cayenne, paprika, red pepper flakes, salt, and black pepper. Toss to combine.

2. Cover and cook on High for 4 to 5 hours or on Low for 8 to 10 hours, until the meat and potatoes are tender.

3. Ladle into bowls, garnish with chopped green onions, and serve.

Butternut Squash Soup

Yield: Serves 6 | Prep Time: 20 minutes | Cook Time: 3–4 hours on High or 6–8 hours on Low

This recipe is a virtual cornucopia of flavors, from fall favorites like butternut squash and apple to a surprise spicy kick with the addition of jalapeño and cayenne pepper. It's a balance between the cozy comforts of the season and the heat of something exciting.

INGREDIENTS

4 pounds butternut squash, peeled, seeded, and cubed

1 Granny Smith apple, peeled, cored, and chopped

1 carrot, chopped

1 jalapeño, seeded and chopped

1 large shallot, chopped

4 garlic cloves, minced

1 tablespoon ground cumin

¼ teaspoon ground nutmeg

⅛ teaspoon cayenne pepper

2 teaspoons kosher salt

½ teaspoon freshly ground black pepper

4 cups chicken broth

1 (14-ounce) can coconut milk

1 tablespoon olive oil

6 fresh sage leaves

Crème fraîche, for serving

DIRECTIONS

1. In a slow cooker, combine the squash, apple, carrot, jalapeño, shallot, garlic, cumin, nutmeg, cayenne, salt, black pepper, and broth.

2. Cover and cook on High for 3 to 4 hours or on Low for 6 to 8 hours, until the squash is tender.

3. Stir in the coconut milk.

4. Carefully transfer to a blender or an immersion blender and puree the soup, working in batches, if desired, to prevent splashing. The soup will be hot.

5. In a small pan, heat the olive oil over medium heat. Add the sage leaves and fry until crispy, about 4 minutes.

6. Ladle the soup into bowls. Dollop the crème fraîche on the soup, top with the fried sage leaves, and serve.

Black Bean Soup

Yield: Serves 8 | Prep Time: 20 minutes | Cook Time: 3–4 hours on High or 6–8 hours on Low

The fiery addition of poblano peppers and jalapeños ratchets up the heat index of this soup, which is soothingly tempered by the smooth sour cream topping. If you're up to the challenge, leave the seeds in the peppers when you chop them for an even spicier touch.

INGREDIENTS

1 onion, diced

1 red bell pepper, seeded and diced

1 green bell pepper, seeded and diced

2 carrots, diced

1 poblano pepper, seeded and chopped

1 jalapeño, seeded and diced

3 garlic cloves, minced

4 (15-ounce) cans black beans, drained and rinsed

1 (14-ounce) can fire-roasted diced tomatoes

1 teaspoon kosher salt

½ teaspoon freshly ground black pepper

½ teaspoon cayenne pepper

1 teaspoon dried oregano

1 tablespoon smoked paprika

1 tablespoon chili powder

1 tablespoon ground cumin

2 bay leaves

4–5 cups vegetable broth

To serve

Lime wedges

Shredded mozzarella cheese

Sour cream

Tortilla chips

DIRECTIONS

1. In a 6-quart slow cooker, combine the onion, bell peppers, carrots, poblano, jalapeño, garlic, black beans, tomatoes, salt, black pepper, cayenne, oregano, paprika, chili powder, cumin, bay leaves, and broth. Stir to combine.

2. Cover and cook on High for 3 to 4 hours or on Low for 6 to 8 hours.

3. Just before the end of cooking, remove the bay leaves and mash up some of the beans.

4. Ladle into bowls and serve with limes, mozzarella, sour cream, and tortilla chips.

Split Pea Soup

Yield: Serves 6–8 | Prep Time: 15 minutes | Cook Time: 3–4 hours on High or 7–8 hours on Low

My aunt is famous in our family for her split pea soup. Her trick is to load it up with plenty of tasty ingredients like ham, celery, and carrots to make each bite worth eating until the bowl's been scraped clean. This is my slow cooker version of that family favorite.

INGREDIENTS

2 cups diced ham steak

1 (16-ounce) package dried green split peas, rinsed

1 large leek, white and light green parts only, chopped and rinsed well

3 celery stalks, diced

2 carrots, diced

2 garlic cloves, minced

¼ cup chopped fresh parsley

2 teaspoons minced fresh thyme

1 teaspoon kosher salt

½ teaspoon freshly ground black pepper

1 bay leaf

6 cups chicken broth

DIRECTIONS

1. In a 6-quart slow cooker, combine the ham steak, split peas, leek, celery, carrots, garlic, parsley, thyme, salt, pepper, bay leaf, and broth. Stir to combine.

2. Cover and cook on High for 3 to 4 hours or on Low for 7 to 8 hours, until the peas are done.

3. Remove the bay leaf, ladle into bowls, and serve.

Cioppino

Yield: Serves 6–8 | Prep Time: 10 minutes | Cook Time: 5 hours on Low

Cioppino is a "catch of the day" type of soup. It typically contains seafood found in the salt water of the Pacific Ocean, such as shrimp, scallops, squid, mussels, and more. Don't be afraid to vary the seafood in this soup depending on your personal preferences.

INGREDIENTS

1 (15-ounce) can diced tomatoes, with their juices

1 red bell pepper, seeded and chopped

1 onion, chopped

3 celery stalks, chopped

2 cups seafood stock

6 ounces tomato paste

½ cup red wine

2 garlic cloves, minced

2 teaspoons Italian seasoning

1 bay leaf

½ teaspoon red pepper flakes

2 (6-ounce) cans solid white albacore tuna in water, drained

1 pound cooked shrimp, peeled and deveined

2 (6-ounce) cans lump crabmeat, drained

1 (6.5-ounce) can chopped clams, drained

2 tablespoons chopped fresh basil

1 tablespoon chopped fresh parsley

Kosher salt and freshly ground black pepper

DIRECTIONS

1. In a 6-quart slow cooker, combine the tomatoes with their juices, bell pepper, onion, celery, stock, tomato paste, wine, garlic, Italian seasoning, bay leaf, and red pepper flakes. Stir to combine.

2. Cover and cook on Low for 5 hours.

3. When ready to serve, remove from the heat and stir in the tuna, shrimp, crabmeat, and clams. Replace the cover and let sit for 5 to 10 minutes, just until the seafood is heated through.

4. Remove the bay leaf and stir in the basil and parsley. Taste and season with salt and black pepper. Ladle into bowls and serve.

3

Main Course Soups

Chicken soups are a memorable part of many childhoods, from sick days to weeknight comforts. And during the colder months of the year, I tend to retreat to a safe haven of beef and pork dishes. In adulthood, soups permeate all corners of my life, whether I'm making Chicken and Wild Rice Soup (page 44) for my in-laws when they come to visit or a spicy Taco Soup (page 71) for a Friday-night indulgence. Soups like these simply deserve to be the stars of the show.

King Ranch Chicken Soup

Yield: Serves 6–8 | Prep Time: 10 minutes | Cook Time: 30 minutes

This soup is even creamier than you'd expect at first glance from the combination of cream cheese, Velveeta cheese, and half-and-half. There's a whole slew of textures in each bite, too, from the crunchy celery and carrots to the soft, diced chicken.

INGREDIENTS

2 tablespoons olive oil

1 onion, finely diced

1 celery stalk, finely diced

1 cup chopped baby carrots

½ red bell pepper, seeded and chopped into bite-size pieces

3 garlic cloves, very finely minced

2 pounds boneless, skinless chicken breasts, cut into 1-inch cubes

1 tablespoon chili powder

1 tablespoon ground cumin

½ teaspoon kosher salt

¼ teaspoon freshly ground black pepper

1 (14-ounce) can kidney beans, drained

1 (14-ounce) can RoTel diced tomatoes with chiles

1 (8-ounce) can tomato sauce

4 cups chicken broth

½ (8-ounce) package cream cheese, cut into small cubes

2 cups Velveeta cheese, cut into small cubes

2 cups half-and-half

Fresh cilantro, for garnish

Lime wedges, for garnish

DIRECTIONS

1. In a large Dutch oven, heat the olive oil over medium-high heat. Add the onion, celery, carrots, bell pepper, and garlic and cook, stirring, for 2 to 3 minutes, until the vegetables are translucent.

2. In a medium bowl, toss together the chicken, chili powder, cumin, salt, and black pepper and add to the pan. Cook, stirring frequently, for about 5 minutes, until the chicken is cooked through.

3. Add the beans, tomatoes with chiles, tomato sauce, and broth and bring to a boil. Reduce the heat to low and simmer for 20 minutes.

4. Remove from the heat and stir in the cream cheese and Velveeta. Return to a simmer and stir until the cheese has melted and the soup is smooth. Remove from the heat once again and stir in the half-and-half. Taste and adjust the seasonings as desired.

5. Ladle into bowls, garnish with cilantro and lime wedges, and serve.

Chicken and Wild Rice Soup

Yield: Serves 4 | Prep Time: 10 minutes | Cook Time: 35 minutes

Wild rice is an underrated ingredient. Not only does it have a distinct toasted, earthy flavor but it also adds textural variety and visual appeal to the dish.

INGREDIENTS

2 tablespoons unsalted butter

1 cup chopped carrot

½ cup chopped celery

½ cup chopped onion

2 cups sliced cremini mushrooms

1 bay leaf

1 tablespoon chopped fresh rosemary, plus additional sprigs for garnish

4 cups low-sodium chicken broth

½ cup uncooked wild rice, rinsed and drained

Kosher salt and freshly ground black pepper

1 cup half-and-half

2 cups shredded cooked chicken (see Note)

DIRECTIONS

1. In a large pot, melt the butter over medium-high heat. Add the carrot, celery, and onion and cook until the vegetables begin to soften and the onions are translucent, about 5 minutes.

2. Add the mushrooms, bay leaf, and rosemary. Stir to combine.

3. Add the broth and wild rice. Bring to a boil and reduce the heat to low. Simmer for 30 minutes, or until the rice is tender but still chewy. Season with salt and pepper.

4. Remove from the heat and stir in the half-and-half. Stir in the chicken and let sit until heated through, about 3 minutes.

5. Remove the bay leaf, ladle into bowls, and serve, garnished with sprigs of rosemary.

NOTE

To cook the chicken, place 2 medium boneless, skinless chicken breasts on a baking sheet and bake at 350°F for 30 minutes.

Turkey Gnocchi Soup

Yield: Serves 4–6 | Prep Time: 15 minutes | Cook Time: 30 minutes

The use of turkey sausage instead of pork sausage makes this soup leaner, while the addition of kale makes this a high-fiber food. If you've never had gnocchi before, it's a soft, doughy dumpling that acts as a potato pillow, complementing the surrounding ingredients, like the turkey sausage.

INGREDIENTS

1 pound Italian turkey sausage

1 onion, diced

4 garlic cloves, minced

4 cups chicken broth

1 jarred roasted red bell pepper, drained and diced

1 pound packaged potato gnocchi

3 cups baby kale, chopped

1 cup heavy cream

⅛ teaspoon ground nutmeg

½ teaspoon kosher salt

¼ teaspoon freshly ground black pepper

Grated Parmesan cheese, for serving

DIRECTIONS

1. In a large pot, cook the turkey sausage and the onion over medium-high heat until the sausage is browned, about 6 minutes. Add the garlic and cook for 1 minute. Drain the excess grease from the pan.

2. Add the broth and the roasted red pepper. Bring to a simmer.

3. Reduce the heat to medium-low and add the gnocchi. Cook for 10 minutes.

4. Stir in the kale, cream, nutmeg, salt, and black pepper. Bring to a simmer and cook until the kale starts to wilt and the soup is heated through.

5. Ladle into bowls and serve topped with Parmesan.

Turkey, Kale, and Rice Soup

Yield: Serves 4–6 | Prep Time: 20 minutes | Cook Time: 30–40 minutes

The tenderness of the cooked kale makes this an ideal soup to enjoy for a weekend lunch. It's filling without being heavy, so you aren't overtired the rest of the day, and the mild seasonings make it palatable for people of all ages.

INGREDIENTS

1 tablespoon olive oil

1 cup diced shallots

3 carrots, sliced

3 celery stalks, sliced

1 red bell pepper, seeded and diced

1 pound ground turkey

¼ teaspoon kosher salt, plus more as needed

¼ teaspoon freshly ground black pepper, plus more as needed

1 teaspoon herbes de Provence

3 garlic cloves, minced

4 cups chicken broth

1 (14-ounce) can fire-roasted diced tomatoes

1 cup cooked white rice (see Note)

4 cups kale, stemmed, leaves chopped

¼ cup chopped fresh parsley, for garnish

Grated Parmesan cheese, for garnish

DIRECTIONS

1. In a large pot, heat the olive oil over medium-high heat. Add the shallots, carrots, celery, and bell pepper and cook, stirring, until softened, about 10 minutes.

2. Add the turkey, season with the salt and black pepper, and cook, stirring, until the turkey is fully cooked, 6 to 7 minutes.

3. Add the herbes de Provence and garlic and cook for 1 minute.

4. Stir in the broth, tomatoes, and rice. Bring to a boil.

5. Add the kale, cover, reduce the heat to low, and simmer for 15 to 20 minutes.

6. Taste and add more salt and pepper, if needed.

7. Ladle into bowls, garnish with parsley and Parmesan, and serve.

NOTE

One-third cup dry rice equals about 1 cup cooked rice.

Chicken Tortilla Soup

Yield: Serves 4–6 | Prep Time: 15 minutes | Cook Time: 30 minutes

Frozen corn allows you to make this soup any time of year. If you'd rather substitute fresh corn from the cob, you may. I used red and black tortilla strips to top the soup since they're just so colorful, but you can use sliced flour or corn tortillas if you prefer.

INGREDIENTS

1 tablespoon olive oil

½ onion, chopped

2 carrots, chopped

1 red bell pepper, seeded and diced

3 garlic cloves, minced

4 cups chicken broth

1 (14.5-ounce) can fire-roasted diced tomatoes

1 tablespoon chili powder

1 canned chipotle in adobo sauce (see Note), finely chopped

1 teaspoon kosher salt

½ teaspoon freshly ground black pepper

1 (2-pound) rotisserie chicken, meat shredded

1 (15-ounce) can black beans, drained and rinsed

1 cup frozen corn kernels

1 tablespoon fresh lime juice

¼ cup fresh chopped cilantro, for garnish

Avocado, sliced, for garnish

Tortilla chips, for serving

DIRECTIONS

1. In a large pot, heat the olive oil over medium heat. Add the onion, carrots, bell pepper, and garlic and cook, stirring, for about 5 minutes, until the onion is translucent.

2. Add the broth, tomatoes, chili powder, chipotle, salt, and black pepper and bring to a boil. Reduce the heat to low and simmer for 10 minutes.

3. Add the chicken, beans, corn, and lime juice. Simmer for 15 to 20 minutes, until the chicken is heated through and the veggies are tender.

4. Ladle into bowls. Garnish with lime juice, cilantro, and avocado and serve with tortilla chips.

NOTE

The chipotle in adobo provides even more spice. Feel free to omit it for a milder heat. The remaining chipotles and sauce in the can freeze very well.

Turkey Dumpling Soup

Yield: Serves 6–8 | Prep Time: 15 minutes | Cook Time: 30–35 minutes

I like to pull out this recipe after Thanksgiving, so I can put all that leftover turkey to use! If you prefer a slightly thicker broth, feel free to add an extra tablespoon of flour in step 2.

INGREDIENTS

3 tablespoons unsalted butter

2 carrots, diced

2 celery stalks, diced

½ cup diced shallots

2 garlic cloves, minced

2 tablespoons all-purpose flour

4 cups chicken broth

1 teaspoon dried sage

1 tablespoon minced fresh thyme

½ teaspoon kosher salt

½ teaspoon freshly ground black pepper

2 bay leaves

2 cups biscuit baking mix

⅔ cup whole milk

2 cups cubed or shredded cooked turkey

1 cup frozen peas

1 cup frozen corn kernels

1 cup heavy cream

DIRECTIONS

1. In a large pot, melt the butter over medium heat. Add the carrots, celery, shallots, and garlic and cook until softened, about 5 minutes.

2. Whisk in the flour. Gradually add in the broth, whisking continuously.

3. Stir in the sage, thyme, salt, pepper, and bay leaves. Bring to a simmer and cook for about 5 minutes.

4. In a medium bowl, mix together the biscuit mix with the milk until well combined.

5. Carefully drop a tablespoon of the dumpling dough at a time into the soup. They will sink initially and then float to the top when they're cooked.

6. Boil for about 5 minutes.

7. Add the turkey, peas, corn, and cream to the soup. Stir to combine and cook until hot, about 4 minutes.

8. Remove the bay leaves, ladle into bowls, and serve.

Egg Drop Soup

Yield: Serves 4 | Prep Time: 5 minutes | Cook Time: 10 minutes

This version of Egg Drop Soup is surprisingly easy to make—and super quick! The better quality your chicken broth, the more flavorful the soup will be. A homemade stock can make this soup much richer.

INGREDIENTS

2 large eggs

1 egg white

4 cups chicken broth

1½ tablespoons cornstarch

¼ teaspoon garlic salt

⅛ teaspoon freshly ground black pepper

½ teaspoon grated fresh ginger (from ⅛ inch piece)

½ teaspoon sesame oil

1 tablespoon soy sauce

½ cup sliced cremini or shiitake mushrooms

4 green onions, sliced, for garnish

DIRECTIONS

1. In a small bowl, whisk together the eggs and egg white. Set aside.

2. In another small bowl, combine ¾ cup of the broth with the cornstarch.

3. Pour the rest of the broth into a medium saucepan and add the garlic salt, pepper, ginger, sesame oil, and soy sauce. Bring to a boil.

4. Add the cornstarch mixture to the pan, stir, and cook for 2 minutes, until thickened. Add the mushrooms.

5. Bring the broth back to a full boil and stir in a clockwise direction.

6. Gently pour the egg mixture into the broth and stir in a clockwise direction for 30 seconds or until the eggs are cooked.

7. Ladle the soup into bowls, garnish with the green onions, and serve.

Old World Peasant Soup

Yield: Serves 5–6 | Prep Time: 15 minutes | Cook Time: 30–35 minutes

I love this kind of soup because the use of sausage and beans makes it an affordable option for dinner. The combination of meat, beans, and veggies gives the dish plenty of texture and flavor, making it a hearty meal to feed a crowd.

INGREDIENTS

1 tablespoon olive oil

1 pound Italian sausage, casing removed, sliced

1 onion, finely chopped

1 carrot, thinly sliced

1 celery stalk, sliced

3 garlic cloves, minced

4 cups chicken broth

2 (15.8-ounce) cans cannellini beans, drained and rinsed

1 (14-ounce) can fire-roasted diced tomatoes

½ teaspoon Italian seasoning

½ teaspoon kosher salt

½ teaspoon freshly ground black pepper

3 cups fresh spinach

Grated Parmesan cheese, for garnish

DIRECTIONS

1. In a large pot, heat the olive oil over medium-high heat. Add the sausage and cook until it's no longer pink.

2. Add the onion, carrot, celery, and garlic and cook until tender, 6 to 8 minutes.

3. Add the broth, beans, tomatoes, Italian seasoning, salt, and pepper. Bring to a boil, then reduce the heat to low and simmer for 20 minutes.

4. Add the spinach and cook for 3 to 4 minutes more.

5. Ladle the soup into bowls and garnish with Parmesan. Serve.

Navy Bean Soup

Yield: Serves 8 | Prep Time: 15 minutes | Cook Time: 20–25 minutes

Navy beans are a fantastic source of fiber, making this a healthy soup to eat for a balanced diet. Another benefit is that navy beans cook relatively quickly compared to cannellini and great northern beans, which makes this soup simple enough to throw together on a weeknight.

INGREDIENTS

1 tablespoon olive oil

½ pound ham steak, cubed

1 cup chopped onion

1 celery stalk, diced

1 carrot, diced

2 garlic cloves, minced

4 (16-ounce) cans navy beans, undrained

3 cups chicken broth

2 teaspoons minced fresh thyme

½ teaspoon kosher salt

½ teaspoon freshly ground black pepper

DIRECTIONS

1. In a large pot, heat the olive oil over medium-high heat. Add the ham, onion, celery, carrot, and garlic and cook, stirring, for 3 to 5 minutes.

2. Stir in the beans with their liquid, broth, thyme, salt, and pepper. Bring to a boil, then reduce the heat to low, cover, and simmer for 10 minutes.

3. Uncover and cook for 5 to 10 minutes more.

4. Ladle into bowls and serve.

Hamburger Soup

Yield: Serves 6 | Prep Time: 15 minutes | Cook Time: 35–40 minutes

I like my burgers with all the fixin's: onion, tomato, cheese, bacon. When I first tried Hamburger Soup, incorporating all those ingredients into one dish, I was in heaven. The buns act like a sponge, soaking in all the flavors, similar to the function of a bread bowl.

INGREDIENTS

1 pound lean ground beef

1 onion, chopped

2 garlic cloves, minced

½ teaspoon kosher salt

½ teaspoon freshly ground black pepper

3½ cups beef broth

1 (28-ounce) can crushed tomatoes

2 tablespoons tomato paste

1 tablespoon Worcestershire sauce

2 hamburger buns, torn into 2-inch pieces

1 cup shredded sharp cheddar cheese

4 bacon slices, cooked and roughly chopped, for garnish

DIRECTIONS

1. In a large pot, cook the ground beef, onion, and garlic. Add the salt and pepper.

2. Add the broth, tomatoes, tomato paste, and Worcestershire sauce and bring to a boil over medium-high heat. Reduce the heat to low and simmer for 20 to 25 minutes.

3. Add the bun pieces and ¾ cup of the cheese and cook for 10 minutes more. The soup should be thick and the buns dissolved.

4. Ladle into bowls. Serve topped with the remaining cheese and the bacon.

30-Minute Beer Cheese Soup

Yield: Serves 4 | Prep Time: 15 minutes | Cook Time: 30 minutes

My husband and I typically watch football games together on Sundays, and I usually bring out something warm for us to chow down on. While chili often makes the cut, this Beer Cheese Soup is another football Sunday favorite.

INGREDIENTS

4 tablespoons (½ stick) unsalted butter

1 celery stalk, chopped

1 shallot, chopped

1 red bell pepper, seeded and chopped

2 garlic cloves, minced

¼ cup all-purpose flour

1 (12-ounce) bottle of beer (any kind, but I use a lager)

1½ cups chicken broth

1 cup heavy cream

2 teaspoons chopped fresh thyme

¼ teaspoon cayenne pepper

4 ounces smoked Gouda cheese, shredded, plus more for serving

4 ounces sharp cheddar cheese, shredded, plus more for serving

¼ teaspoon kosher salt

¼ teaspoon freshly ground black pepper

3 bacon slices, cooked and crumbled, for garnish

Chopped fresh chives, for garnish

Garlic bread, for serving

DIRECTIONS

1. In a large pot, melt the butter over medium-high heat. Add the celery, shallot, bell pepper, and garlic. Cook for about 5 minutes, until the vegetables have softened.

2. Stir in the flour and mix until the vegetables are coated.

3. Add the beer, broth, cream, thyme, and cayenne. Bring to a boil, then reduce the heat to medium. Cook for 15 minutes.

4. Remove from the heat and stir in the Gouda and cheddar cheeses until they are fully melted.

5. Season with the salt and black pepper.

6. Ladle into bowls and top the soup with additional cheese, the bacon, and chives. Serve with garlic bread.

NOTES

To make garlic bread, mix 1 chopped garlic clove with ⅓ cup room-temperature butter. Cut a loaf of French bread into 1-inch slices and spread the butter mixture on one side of each piece. Reassemble the loaf and wrap in aluminum foil. Bake in a 400°F oven for 15 to 20 minutes.

Jambalaya

Yield: Serves 6–8 | Prep Time: 20 minutes | Cook Time: 45–50 minutes

Jambalaya, which comes from the Provençal word *jambalaia*, meaning "mix up," among other potential interpretations, originated in southern Louisiana. Any variation or combination of meats is acceptable to use in jambalaya, but I love this hodgepodge of sausage, chicken, and shrimp.

INGREDIENTS

3 tablespoons olive oil

2 celery stalks, chopped

1 onion, diced

1 red bell pepper, seeded and diced

1 yellow bell pepper, seeded and diced

1 green bell pepper, seeded and diced

1 jalapeño, seeded and minced

4 garlic cloves, minced

2 boneless, skinless chicken thighs, cut into bite-size pieces

1 pound andouille sausage, cut into rounds

3 cups chicken broth

1 (14-ounce) can fire-roasted diced tomatoes

1½ cups uncooked white rice

2 tablespoons Cajun or Creole seasoning

1 bay leaf

1 teaspoon minced fresh thyme

¼ teaspoon cayenne pepper

½ teaspoon red pepper flakes

2 tablespoons Worcestershire sauce

1 pound raw shrimp, peeled and deveined

½ teaspoon kosher salt

½ teaspoon freshly ground black pepper

Hot sauce, for garnish

Green onions, sliced, for garnish

DIRECTIONS

1. In a large pot, heat 2 tablespoons of the olive oil over medium-high heat. Add the celery, onion, bell peppers, jalapeño, and garlic and cook, stirring, for about 5 minutes.

2. Add the remaining 1 tablespoon olive oil, the chicken, and the sausage and cook for 5 minutes more, until the chicken is no longer pink.

3. Add the broth, tomatoes, rice, Cajun seasoning, bay leaf, thyme, cayenne, red pepper flakes, and Worcestershire sauce.

4. Reduce the heat to low and simmer, stirring occasionally, for 25 to 30 minutes.

5. When the rice is tender, add the shrimp and simmer until the shrimp are fully cooked and pink, 5 to 8 minutes.

6. Remove the bay leaf and add the salt and black pepper.

7. Ladle into bowls and garnish with the hot sauce and green onions. Serve.

Beefy Nacho Soup

Yield: Serves 4 | Prep Time: 10 minutes | Cook Time: 20 minutes

One of my favorite cooking shortcuts is using seasoning mixes. You get the perfect mixture of seasonings without needing to dig through your spice cabinet. I use Old El Paso taco seasoning mix in this recipe. I've also used ranch dressing mix in the Slow Cooker Creamy Chicken Stew (page 167) and the Slow Cooker Buffalo Chicken Chili (page 192).

INGREDIENTS

1 pound ground beef

1½ cups half-and-half

1 (15-ounce) can black beans, drained and rinsed

1 (10¾-ounce) can condensed nacho cheese soup

1 (10-ounce) can Ro-Tel diced tomatoes and green chiles, undrained

1 tablespoon Old El Paso taco seasoning mix (from a 1-ounce package)

½ cup shredded sharp cheddar cheese, for serving

Sour cream, for serving

Diced avocado, for serving

DIRECTIONS

1. In a medium saucepan, brown the ground beef over medium-high heat, about 8 minutes. Drain the grease.

2. Reduce the heat to medium. Stir in the half-and-half, black beans, nacho cheese soup, diced tomatoes and green chiles, and taco seasoning. Cook for 8 to 12 minutes, until heated through.

3. Ladle into bowls and top with cheddar cheese, sour cream, and avocado. Serve.

Cheesesteak Soup

Yield: Serves 4 | Prep Time: 30 minutes | Cook Time: 45–50 minutes

One of my close friends was moving to Philadelphia, and I was planning to throw her a bon voyage dinner to see her off. She had talked so much about her anticipation for her first authentic Philly cheesesteak that I wanted to surprise her with a soup version, complete with plenty of melted provolone cheese.

INGREDIENTS

3 tablespoons olive oil

2 thick slices sourdough bread, cubed

1 teaspoon finely minced garlic

2 carrots, chopped

1 small onion, chopped

8 ounces cremini mushrooms, sliced

1–2 teaspoons finely minced fresh thyme

⅓ cup all-purpose flour

4 cups beef broth

1 tablespoon Worcestershire sauce

1 teaspoon hot sauce

5 ounces sharp cheddar cheese, shredded

5 ounces provolone cheese, shredded, plus 1 cup shredded provolone for garnish

1 pound top round steak, thinly sliced

1 green bell pepper, seeded and sliced into strips

DIRECTIONS

1. In a medium bowl, toss 1 tablespoon of the olive oil with the sourdough bread cubes and garlic. Put the bread cubes in a small skillet and cook over medium-high heat until browned and crispy. Set aside.

2. In a large pot, heat 1 tablespoon olive oil over medium-high heat. Add the carrots, onion, and mushrooms and cook until the vegetables are soft. Add the thyme and stir.

3. Add the flour and cook for 3 to 4 minutes, being careful not to burn the flour. Add the broth, Worcestershire sauce, and hot sauce. Reduce to medium-low and simmer for about 15 minutes.

4. Preheat the oven to broil. Carefully transfer the soup to a blender and puree until smooth. (Alternatively, blend the soup directly in the pot using an immersion blender.)

5. Return the soup to the pot (if necessary) and bring to a boil over medium-high heat. Remove the soup from the heat and stir in the cheddar and provolone cheeses until melted.

6. In a large skillet, heat the remaining 1 tablespoon olive oil over medium-high heat. Add the top round steak and bell pepper and cook until the beef is browned and the peppers are softened.

7. Divide the beef and peppers among four broiler-safe soup bowls. Add some of the bread cubes and top with the hot soup. Sprinkle each bowl with some of the provolone. Broil until the cheese melts, about 4 minutes. Serve immediately.

Taco Soup

Yield: Serves 4–6 | Prep Time: 10 minutes | Cook Time: 30 minutes

Taco night is taken to a whole other level when this soup comes into play. The black beans add a sweet, mild taste to the dish while the kidney beans take on an earthier flavor. The combination of the two creates an ideal taco substitute.

INGREDIENTS

1 tablespoon olive oil

1 pound lean ground beef

1 (1-ounce) packet Old El Paso taco seasoning

1 tablespoon dried oregano

Kosher salt and freshly ground black pepper

1 cup water

1 red bell pepper, seeded and diced

½ onion, diced

1 (4-ounce) can diced green chiles

1 (15-ounce) can kidney beans, drained and rinsed

1 (15-ounce) can black beans, drained and rinsed

1 (10-ounce) can RoTel tomatoes and green chiles

1 cup frozen corn kernels

2 cups chicken broth, preferably low-sodium

Taco fixings, for serving (chopped red onion, chopped tomato, sliced jalapeño, and chopped cilantro)

DIRECTIONS

1. In a large skillet, heat the olive oil over medium-high heat. Add the ground beef and begin to brown. Add the taco seasoning, oregano, salt, and black pepper while browning the meat. Add 1 cup water and simmer until the water evaporates, stirring often, about 10 minutes.

2. When the meat is cooked through, add the bell pepper and onion. Cook, stirring, for 5 minutes until the veggies are softened.

3. Add the green chiles, kidney beans, black beans, tomatoes with chiles, corn, and broth. Bring to a boil, then reduce the heat to low and simmer for 10 to 15 minutes.

4. Remove from the heat and let cool for 10 minutes before serving.

5. Ladle into bowls and serve topped with your favorite taco fixings.

Worth the Wait Cabbage Soup

Yield: Serves 12 | Prep Time: 20 minutes | Cook Time: 1½–2 hours

Cabbage is both a nourishing and inexpensive way to feed a large group of people. The secret to this recipe is the addition of light brown sugar. It adds a sweetness to the dish that prevents the cabbage from tasting too bland.

INGREDIENTS

1 tablespoon olive oil

½ red onion, chopped

2 carrots, sliced

2 garlic cloves, minced

8 cups chopped green cabbage

8 cups beef broth

2 (28-ounce) cans crushed tomatoes

1 (6-ounce) can tomato paste

⅓ cup packed light brown sugar

1 tablespoon Worcestershire sauce

3–4 sprigs thyme

1 teaspoon kosher salt, plus more as needed

½ teaspoon freshly ground black pepper, plus more as needed

1–2 teaspoons balsamic vinegar

DIRECTIONS

1. In a large pot, heat the olive oil over medium-high heat. Add the onion, carrots, and garlic and cook for 5 minutes.

2. Stir in the cabbage, broth, tomatoes, tomato paste, brown sugar, Worcestershire sauce, thyme, salt, and pepper. Bring to a boil, then reduce the heat to low and simmer for 1½ to 2 hours, until the vegetables are tender.

3. Add the vinegar and more salt and pepper, if needed. Remove the thyme sprigs.

4. Ladle into bowls and serve.

Cream of Broccoli–Cheese Soup

Yield: Serves 6–8 | Prep Time: 10 minutes | Cook Time: 30 minutes

I like to think of this as my "naughty and nice" soup recipe. There's broccoli with all those good-for-you nutrients, paired with melty, creamy cheese for a hint of indulgence.

INGREDIENTS

2 tablespoons unsalted butter

1 onion, finely diced

3 sprigs fresh thyme

2 garlic cloves, finely minced

Kosher salt and freshly ground black pepper

2 (10-ounce) packages chopped frozen broccoli, thawed

3 tablespoons all-purpose flour

3 cups chicken broth

1½ cups heavy cream

2 cups shredded cheddar cheese

DIRECTIONS

1. In a large pot, melt the butter over medium heat. Add the onion and thyme. Stir and cook until the onion is translucent. Add the garlic and season with salt and pepper. Add the broccoli and then sprinkle flour over everything. Stir to combine and cook until all the flour has been absorbed. Slowly pour the broth over the mixture and stir to combine and smooth any lumps. Increase the heat to medium-high and bring to a boil for 3 to 5 minutes.

2. Reduce the heat to low and simmer for 10 to 15 minutes, until the broccoli is tender. Stir in the cream and cheddar cheese. Remove from the heat, taste, and adjust the seasoning if necessary.

3. Remove the thyme stems, ladle into bowls, and serve.

Roasted Cauliflower Cheddar Soup

Yield: Serves 4 | Prep Time: 15–20 minutes | Cook Time: 50–60 minutes

Roasted vegetables are severely underrated. In my opinion, they are the easiest and tastiest way to get anyone to eat a well-balanced meal. By adding them to this soup, there's a crisp, slightly smoky flavor that contrasts well against the melted cheddar cheese.

INGREDIENTS

1 head cauliflower, cut into florets (about 4 cups)

6 garlic cloves

3 tablespoons olive oil

¼ teaspoon kosher salt, plus more as needed

¼ teaspoon freshly ground black pepper, plus more as needed

2 shallots, diced

1 teaspoon minced fresh thyme

1 teaspoon minced fresh rosemary

¼ teaspoon ground nutmeg

3 cups chicken broth

1½ cups shredded aged white cheddar cheese

1 cup heavy cream

¼ cup shredded Parmesan cheese, for garnish

4 bacon slices, cooked and crumbled, for garnish

DIRECTIONS

1. Preheat the oven to 400°F.

2. In a medium bowl, toss the cauliflower, garlic, 2 tablespoons of the olive oil, the salt, and the pepper. Place on a baking sheet and roast for 25 to 30 minutes, until golden.

3. In a large pot, heat the remaining 1 tablespoon olive oil over medium heat. Add the shallots and cook for 6 to 8 minutes, until tender. Add the thyme, rosemary, and nutmeg and cook for 1 minute.

4. Add the broth, then the cauliflower and garlic. Bring to a boil, reduce the heat to low, and cook for 20 minutes.

5. Carefully transfer the soup to a blender and puree until smooth. (Alternatively, puree the soup directly in the pot with an immersion blender.) Return the pureed soup to the pot (if necessary), stir in the cheddar, and let it melt over low heat.

6. Stir in the cream. Season with some salt and pepper.

7. Ladle into bowls, garnish with the Parmesan and bacon, and serve.

Provençal Vegetable Soup

Yield: Serves 4–6 | Prep Time: 15 minutes | Cook Time: 45 minutes

Provençal Vegetable Soup is characterized by the basil-pesto topping, which adds a burst of herbal flavor to your bowl. I've added some chicken to give the dish more protein, but feel free to omit it and use vegetable broth for a vegetarian version.

INGREDIENTS

3 tablespoons light olive oil

1 boneless, skinless chicken breast, cubed (optional; see Notes)

Kosher salt and freshly ground black pepper

1 large onion, chopped

2 garlic cloves, minced

1 red bell pepper, seeded and diced

1 cup chopped carrots

1 cup chopped celery

4 ounces cremini mushrooms

1 zucchini, chopped

¼ cup chopped fresh parsley

2 tablespoons herbes de Provence

1 bay leaf

½ cup white wine

6 cups chicken broth

1 (15-ounce) can cannellini beans, undrained

8 baby red potatoes, quartered

Prepared basil pesto, for serving (see Notes)

DIRECTIONS

1. In a large pot, heat the olive oil over medium heat. Add the chicken (if using) and lightly brown on all sides. Season with salt and black pepper. Add the onion, garlic, bell pepper, carrots, celery, mushrooms, and zucchini. Stir to combine. Add the parsley, herbes de Provence, and bay leaf. Cook, stirring, until the vegetables are tender, about 5 to 7 minutes. Season lightly with salt and black pepper.

2. Deglaze the pan with the wine by pouring the wine in and stirring while scraping up any browned bits from the bottom of the pan. Simmer until the wine has reduced by half, about 8 minutes.

3. Stir in the broth and add the cannellini beans and potatoes. Simmer for about 15 minutes, until the potatoes are tender.

4. Remove from the heat and discard the bay leaf. Taste and adjust the seasoning.

5. Ladle the soup into large bowls. Serve with a heaping tablespoon of pesto on top. Stir the pesto into the soup as you eat.

NOTES

To cook the chicken, place 1 medium boneless, skinless chicken breast on a baking sheet and bake at 350°F for 30 minutes.

To make the basil pesto, combine 2 cups fresh basil leaves, 3 garlic cloves, and ¼ cup pine nuts in a food processor and pulse. Add ⅔ cup olive oil and ½ cup shredded Parmesan cheese. Add kosher salt and freshly ground black pepper. Blend and serve.

Jalapeño Popper Soup

Yield: Serves 4–6 | Prep Time: 5 minutes | Cook Time: 20 minutes

The combination of jalapeños and cream cheese creates the spicy-cheesy dynamic that the bite-size appetizers have perfected. The biggest difference here is that I'm able to add some veggies like onion, celery, and carrot to add a more dynamic range of flavors.

INGREDIENTS

½ cup (1 stick) unsalted butter

1 onion, finely diced

2 large celery stalks, chopped

1 large carrot, chopped

4 garlic cloves, minced

1 (12-ounce) jar jalapeño slices, undrained

¼ cup all-purpose flour

2 cups low-sodium chicken broth

2 cups whole milk

1 (8-ounce) package cream cheese, cubed

Kosher salt and freshly ground black pepper

Shredded cheddar cheese, for garnish

4–6 slices bacon, cooked and crumbled, for garnish

DIRECTIONS

1. In a large pot, melt the butter over medium heat. Add the onion, celery, carrot, garlic, and jalapeño slices (reserve a few for garnish, and reserve the juice) and cook, stirring, until tender, about 10 minutes.

2. When the vegetables are tender, add the flour and stir until all the flour has been absorbed. Cook for 2 minutes, until the mixture is heated through and turns a light golden color.

3. Add the broth to the flour mixture, stirring vigorously to avoid lumps.

4. Slowly stir in the milk and jarred jalapeño juices. Bring the mixture to a simmer, stirring frequently, for about 20 minutes. The soup will thicken as it cooks.

5. Add the cream cheese, salt, and pepper and stir until melted and combined. Remove from the heat.

6. Ladle into bowls and serve topped with cheddar cheese, bacon, and reserved jalapeño slices.

Mexican Chicken Lime Soup

Yield: Serves 4–6 | Prep Time: 10 minutes | Cook Time: 1 hour 10 minutes

This soup has everything you could want in a flavorful soup: it's savory, a little bit tangy, and a touch spicy. All I need is a side of chips and guacamole, and the meal's complete!

INGREDIENTS

1 tablespoon olive oil

1 onion, diced

2 celery stalks, diced

1 jalapeño, seeded and diced, plus sliced jalapeño for garnish

4 garlic cloves, minced

1 pound boneless, skinless chicken breast

7 cups chicken broth

1 (10-ounce) can RoTel tomatoes with chilies

1 teaspoon dried oregano

1½ teaspoons ground cumin

1 lime, halved, plus lime wheels for garnish

½ bunch cilantro, chopped

DIRECTIONS

1. In a large pot, heat the olive oil over medium heat. Add the onion, celery, jalapeño, and garlic and cook for about 5 minutes, or until the onion is translucent.

2. Add the chicken breast, broth, RoTel tomatoes, oregano, and cumin. Stir well and bring to a boil over high heat. Reduce the heat to low, cover, and simmer gently for 1 hour.

3. Carefully remove the chicken breast from the pot and shred the meat with two forks. Return the meat to the pot. Squeeze the lime juice into the soup and add the cilantro. Stir to combine.

4. Ladle into bowls. Garnish with sliced jalapeños and lime wheels and serve.

Mexican Pozole

Yield: Serves 6 | Prep Time: 15 minutes | Cook Time: 1 hour

Pozole is often served on special occasions, like weddings and birthdays. There are three different kinds of pozole: green, red, and white. The green version includes a rich sauce using ingredients such as tomatillos or jalapeños. The red version, like the one here, uses a sauce with chiles, while the white version goes without either sauce.

INGREDIENTS

3 tablespoons olive oil

1 pound pork loin, cut into bite-size pieces

1 cup chopped onion

3 garlic cloves, minced

1 poblano pepper, chopped

5 cups chicken broth

1 (14.5-ounce) can red enchilada sauce

1 (4.5-ounce) can chopped green chiles

1 teaspoon ancho chile powder

1 teaspoon chili powder

1 teaspoon ground cumin

½ teaspoon oregano

½ teaspoon smoked paprika

2 bay leaves

1 (15.5-ounce) can white hominy, drained

1 tablespoon fresh lime juice

½ cup chopped fresh cilantro

Sliced radishes, for garnish

Fried tortilla strips (homemade or store-bought), for garnish

Lime wedges, for garnish

Diced avocado, for garnish

DIRECTIONS

1. In a large pot, heat the olive oil over medium heat. Add the pork, onion, garlic, and poblano. Sear the pork on all sides, 8 to 10 minutes.

2. Stir in the broth, enchilada sauce, chiles, both chili powders, cumin, oregano, paprika, and bay leaves.

3. Bring to a boil. Reduce the heat to low, cover, and simmer for 40 minutes.

4. Stir in the hominy. Cover and cook for 10 minutes.

5. Remove the bay leaves. Stir in the lime juice and cilantro.

6. Ladle into bowls. Top with the radishes, tortilla strips, lime wedges, and avocado and serve.

Sweet-and-Sour Soup

Yield: Serves 4 | Prep Time: 30 minutes | Cook Time: 10 minutes

While I've ordered this dish from takeout restaurants many times before, there's something so pure about trying the first bowl of a freshly made batch. Maybe it's just the pride of knowing I made it myself, but I always think it tastes so much better. The bright and crunchy bamboo shoots add wonderful texture, too.

INGREDIENTS

4 cups chicken broth

4 ounces shiitake mushrooms, thinly sliced

1 (8-ounce) can bamboo shoots, drained and thinly sliced

8 ounces firm tofu, drained and cut into ¼-inch strips

2 garlic cloves, grated

2 teaspoons grated fresh ginger

1 tablespoon balsamic vinegar

3 tablespoons rice vinegar

1 tablespoon Sriracha sauce

3 tablespoons soy sauce

2 teaspoons light brown sugar

2 tablespoons cornstarch, mixed with 2 tablespoons cold water

2 large eggs, lightly beaten

2 teaspoons toasted sesame oil

1 teaspoon freshly ground white pepper

4 green onions, thinly sliced

1 cup shredded barbecued pork (see Notes)

DIRECTIONS

1. In a large saucepan, combine the broth, mushrooms, bamboo shoots, tofu, garlic, ginger, balsamic vinegar, rice vinegar, Sriracha, soy sauce, and brown sugar. Bring to a boil, then reduce the heat to low and simmer for 5 minutes.

2. Add the cornstarch mixture and cook for 2 minutes.

3. While stirring clockwise, slowly drizzle the eggs over the soup.

4. Stir in the sesame oil, white pepper, and green onions.

5. Add the pork and mix in.

6. Ladle into bowls and serve.

VARIATIONS

You can use vegetable broth instead of chicken broth, substitute another type of mushroom, or use shredded barbecued chicken instead of pork.

NOTES

If you want a slightly more sour soup, add a bit more vinegar; if you want a hotter soup, add more white pepper.

We used premade barbecued pork from the grocery store. You can find it in your grocer's deli aisle.

Thai Coconut Chicken Soup

Yield: Serves 4 | Prep Time: 20 minutes | Cook Time: 20 minutes

My favorite part about this soup is the addition of sweet coconut milk. The broth of the soup becomes thicker and creamier, making it a very comforting option. The hint of lime juice adds a distinct tang, too.

INGREDIENTS

2 teaspoons olive oil

1 cup sliced cremini mushrooms

½ cup chopped red bell pepper

1 carrot, shredded

4 teaspoons minced fresh ginger

4 garlic cloves, minced

1 (3-inch) stalk lemongrass, halved lengthwise

2 teaspoons sambal oelek (chile paste; see Notes)

3 cups chicken broth

1¼ cups light coconut milk

4 teaspoons fish sauce

1 tablespoon sugar

2 cups shredded cooked chicken breasts (see Notes)

1 cup cooked white rice (see Notes)

½ cup green onions, chopped (about 1 bunch)

3 tablespoons chopped fresh basil

2 tablespoons fresh lime juice

DIRECTIONS

1. In a large pot, heat the olive oil over medium heat. Add the mushrooms, bell pepper, carrot, ginger, garlic, and lemongrass. Stir and cook for 3 minutes.

2. Stir in the sambal oelek, then add the broth, coconut milk, fish sauce, and sugar. Bring to a simmer, reduce the heat to low, and cook for 10 minutes.

3. Add the chicken and cooked rice to the pot and cook for about 3 minutes, until fully heated through.

4. Discard the lemongrass. Add the green onions, basil, and lime juice. Stir to combine.

5. Ladle into bowls and serve.

NOTES

If you wish, substitute Sriracha for the sambal oelek.

To cook the chicken, place 2 medium boneless, skinless chicken breasts on a baking sheet and bake at 350°F for 30 minutes. Shred.

One-third cup dry rice equals about 1 cup cooked rice.

Thai Shrimp Soup

Yield: Serves 6 | Prep Time: 15 minutes | Cook Time: 20 minutes

This is similar to the famous Thai soup *tom yum*. If you're not a fan of shrimp, you can easily substitute chicken or pork. If you want to substitute one of the veggies, you can do that as well! Once you have the basics down, feel free to play. Just make sure you leave in the lemongrass to give the dish its delicate citrus flavor.

INGREDIENTS

1 cup uncooked basmati rice

2 tablespoons unsalted butter

1 pound raw shrimp, peeled and deveined

½ teaspoon kosher salt

¼ teaspoon freshly ground black pepper

2 garlic cloves, minced

1 onion, diced

1 red bell pepper, seeded and diced

1 tablespoon grated fresh ginger

1 lemongrass stalk, halved lengthwise

2 tablespoons red curry paste

2 (12-ounce) cans unsweetened coconut milk

4 cups chicken broth

1 tablespoon light brown sugar

1 tablespoon soy sauce

Juice of 1 lime

2 tablespoons torn fresh basil leaves

DIRECTIONS

1. In a medium pot, combine 1½ cups water and the rice and cook according to the package instructions. Set aside.

2. In a large pot, melt the butter over medium-high heat. Add the shrimp, salt, and black pepper. Heat until the shrimp are cooked, about 3 minutes. Remove the shrimp and set aside.

3. Put the garlic, onion, and bell pepper in the pot and cook for 3 to 4 minutes.

4. Stir in the ginger and lemongrass and cook for 1 minute.

5. Whisk in the curry paste, then stir in the coconut milk, broth, brown sugar, and soy sauce.

6. Bring the mixture to a boil, reduce the heat to low, and cook for 8 to 10 minutes. Remove the lemongrass.

7. Stir in the rice, shrimp, lime juice, and basil. Ladle into bowls and serve.

Easy Homemade Wonton Soup

Yield: Serves 8 | Prep Time: 30–40 minutes | Cook Time: 20 minutes

Homemade wontons are so much fun to make. It's as though you're wrapping up these bite-size presents to bestow on your dinner party.

INGREDIENTS

Wontons

1 pound ground pork

2 teaspoons grated fresh ginger

2 teaspoons soy sauce

2 teaspoons sesame oil

⅓ cup thinly sliced green onions

Kosher salt and freshly ground black pepper

1 (12-ounce) package wonton wrappers

½ pound peeled cooked shrimp, chopped

Soup

2 teaspoons sesame oil

2 garlic cloves, minced

1 teaspoon grated fresh ginger

7 cups chicken broth

4 ounces shiitake mushrooms, chopped

2–3 large carrots, shredded (about ½ cup)

3 leaves bok choy, coarsely chopped

½ cup thinly sliced green onions, for garnish

Soy sauce, for garnish

DIRECTIONS

1. *For the wontons:* In a food processor, combine the pork, ginger, soy sauce, sesame oil, and green onions and season with salt and pepper. Mix until thoroughly combined.

2. Place a wonton wrapper on a clean cutting board. Place a walnut-size portion of the meat filling in the center of the wrapper and top with a small amount of chopped shrimp. Moisten the wrapper with water around the edges. Bring two opposite corners together at a point, then seal the rest of the sides tightly, forming a triangle and squeezing out as much air as possible.

3. With one point facing you, pull the two opposite corners toward each other to form the triangle into classic wonton shape, using a little water to seal the edges. Place on a baking sheet in a single layer and repeat with the remaining wontons. Freeze any leftover wontons you do not plan to use in this batch of soup.

4. Bring a large pot of water to boil. Working in batches as needed, boil the wontons for 3 to 5 minutes, until the center is no longer pink. Transfer the wontons to a large bowl once cooked.

5. *For the soup:* In a large pot, heat the sesame oil over medium heat.

6. Add the garlic and ginger and cook, stirring, until fragrant, about 1 minute. Stir in the broth, mushrooms, and carrots. Bring to a boil and cook for 10 minutes, until the mushrooms have softened. Add the bok choy and cook for 3 to 4 minutes, until the greens are wilted.

7. Divide the wontons among eight bowls. Ladle the soup over the top. Garnish with green onions and a drizzle of soy sauce. Serve.

NOTES

Keep the wontons covered with a towel while working, pulling them out one at a time to keep them from drying out. Avoid overfilling the wontons, as they will burst as the filling expands.

This recipe makes plenty of extra wontons. Prepare as directed and freeze the extras before boiling. To use, simply toss frozen wontons right into the soup and simmer for 10 to 15 minutes, or until cooked through.

"Crab" and Wild Rice Soup

Yield: Serves 4 | Prep Time: 5 minutes | Cook Time: 20 minutes

Imitation crab is a handy ingredient to use in a dish like this where its seafood appeal is melded with many other flavors. It's way less expensive than actual crab—plus, it's lower in fat and calories.

INGREDIENTS

6 tablespoons (¾ stick) unsalted butter

1 cup uncooked wild rice, rinsed and drained

1 small onion, diced

2 garlic cloves, minced

4 cups low-sodium vegetable broth

Kosher salt

1 cup frozen carrots and peas

1 cup frozen corn kernels

1 (8-ounce) bag imitation crab, coarsely chopped

½ teaspoon dried thyme

Freshly ground black pepper

¼ cup all-purpose flour

1 cup 2% milk

½ cup heavy cream

DIRECTIONS

1. In a large pot, heat 2 tablespoons of the butter over medium-high heat. Add the rice, onion, and garlic. Cook, stirring, until the rice begins to smell nutty, being careful not to burn the garlic. Add the broth and a pinch of salt. Cover and cook over low heat for 30 minutes, or until the rice is soft.

2. Add the frozen vegetables, imitation crab, and thyme and season with salt and pepper. Cook for 15 minutes more.

3. Meanwhile, in a medium saucepan, melt the remaining 4 tablespoons butter over medium heat. Sprinkle in the flour and whisk continuously until the flour has been absorbed and the mixture is very pale. Whisk in the milk and stir vigorously to ensure there are no lumps. Stir in the cream. Season with a dash of salt and pepper. Bring to a boil and cook for 5 minutes, until the mixture begins to thicken. Pour into the pot and stir to combine.

4. Serve immediately.

Bouillabaisse

Yield: Serves 4 | Prep Time: 10 minutes | Cook Time: 45 minutes

When I was studying in France, this was the Holy Grail of recipes. Mastering the perfect bouillabaisse meant reaching a new echelon of French cooking. After a few tries, this was my favorite version of the dish.

INGREDIENTS

Aioli

1 garlic clove, very finely minced

½ teaspoon kosher salt

Pinch of saffron

¼ cup mayonnaise

Juice of ½ lemon

Bouillabaisse

2 tablespoons olive oil, plus more for brushing

2 garlic cloves, minced

½ fennel bulb, thinly sliced, a handful of fronds reserved

¾ cup white wine

1 (28-ounce) can whole peeled tomatoes

1 bunch basil, plus more for garnish

3 cups seafood stock

Kosher salt and freshly ground black pepper

2 snapper fillets, cut into large chunks

2 tilapia fillets, cut into large chunks

½ pound jumbo shrimp

2 pounds mussels, cleaned and debearded

4 (¾-inch-thick) slices crusty bread

1 lemon, quartered, for serving

Fresh parsley, for garnish

DIRECTIONS

1. *For the aioli:* On a cutting board, mash the garlic and salt together. Keep mashing until a fine paste forms. In a small bowl, combine the garlic paste, saffron, mayonnaise, and lemon juice. Cover and refrigerate until ready to use.

2. *For the bouillabaisse:* In a large pot, heat the olive oil over medium-high heat. Add the garlic and sliced fennel bulb and cook, stirring, until fragrant. Add the wine and simmer for 5 to 8 minutes to reduce the liquid. Add the tomatoes, basil, fennel fronds, and seafood stock. Simmer, stirring occasionally and breaking up the tomatoes, for 15 to 20 minutes, until the liquid has reduced further.

3. Turn off the heat. Puree the soup using an immersion blender until smooth. Taste and season with salt and pepper.

4. Reheat the liquid in the same pot and add the fish, largest pieces first. Add the shrimp and mussels. Very gently, stir to bring some liquid to the top. Cover and cook gently over medium-low heat for about 5 minutes, or until all the mussels have opened up and the shrimp turns pink. (Discard any mussels that don't open.)

5. Heat a small skillet over medium-high heat. Brush both sides of the bread with olive oil and toast each side until lightly golden brown. Generously smear the warm bread with the aioli.

6. Ladle the soup into bowls. Coarsely chop a few basil leaves and garnish the soup. Add a slice of saffron aioli toast to each bowl and serve with lemon wedges and fresh parsley.

Avgolemono

Yield: Serves 4 | Prep Time: 10 minutes | Cook Time: 1 hour 15 minutes

The first time I tried Avgolemono, I was exploring the Greek countryside with my husband, and we stopped in a tiny restaurant on the side of the road. No one was there except for us, the owners, and their three dogs. When I asked for the daily special, this light yet creamy veggie and chicken soup came out. I knew I'd have to make a version for myself as soon as we came home.

INGREDIENTS

2 tablespoons extra-virgin olive oil

1 onion, diced

2 pounds boneless, skinless chicken breasts

7 cups low-sodium chicken broth

2 carrots, finely chopped

2 celery stalks, chopped

1 bay leaf

1½ cups orzo pasta

½ cup fresh lemon juice (from 3 or 4 lemons)

4 large eggs

Kosher salt and freshly ground black pepper

Lemon wedges, for garnish

DIRECTIONS

1. In a large pot, heat the olive oil over medium heat. Add the onion and cook until translucent, about 5 minutes.

2. Add the chicken, broth, carrots, celery, and bay leaf to the pot. Bring to a gentle boil and cook until the chicken is cooked through, about 1 hour. Remove the chicken from the pot, shred the meat with two forks, and return it to the pot.

3. Return the broth to a boil and add the orzo. Boil until the orzo is cooked according to the package directions.

4. Measure 2 cups of the broth out of the pan and set aside.

5. In a small bowl, beat the lemon juice and eggs together. Slowly stir in the reserved broth, whisking continuously. Pour the egg mixture into the pot, stirring well.

6. Taste and season with salt and pepper. Remove the bay leaf.

7. Ladle into bowls, garnish with lemon wedges, and serve.

Swedish Meatball Noodle Soup

Yield: Serves 6 | Prep Time: 30 minutes | Cook Time: 45 minutes

This recipe capitalizes on the sweet, earthy flavor of the meatballs, due to the additions of heavy cream and nutmeg.

INGREDIENTS

Meatballs

1 cup soft bread crumbs

½ cup heavy cream

½ onion, minced

1 pound lean ground beef

1 large egg

1 teaspoon kosher salt

1 teaspoon garlic powder

½ teaspoon freshly ground black pepper

¼ teaspoon ground nutmeg

¼ teaspoon ground allspice

2 tablespoons olive oil

Soup

1 cup heavy cream

2 tablespoons cornstarch

5 tablespoons unsalted butter

2 carrots, thinly sliced

2 celery stalks, chopped

8 ounces cremini mushrooms, sliced

4 garlic cloves, minced

½ cup all-purpose flour

7 cups beef broth

1 teaspoon Worcestershire sauce

1 teaspoon kosher salt, plus more as needed

½ teaspoon smoked paprika

½ teaspoon freshly ground black pepper, plus more as needed

¼ teaspoon red pepper flakes

1 cup frozen peas, thawed

½ cup sour cream

8 ounces egg noodles, cooked to al dente

DIRECTIONS

1. *For the meatballs:* In a large bowl, combine the bread crumbs, cream, onion, ground beef, egg, salt, garlic powder, pepper, nutmeg, and allspice. Form the meat mixture into tablespoon-size meatballs.

2. Line a baking sheet with paper towels. In a large skillet, heat the olive oil over medium heat. Working in batches, brown the meatballs on all sides. Place them on the baking sheet.

3. *For the soup:* In a small bowl, mix the heavy cream and cornstarch. Set aside.

4. In a large pot, melt the butter over medium heat. Add the carrots, celery, and mushrooms and cook for 3 minutes. Add the garlic and cook for another minute. Sprinkle in the flour and cook, stirring continuously, until it has been completely absorbed.

5. Reduce the heat to low and slowly add the broth and heavy cream mixture. Add the Worcestershire sauce, salt, paprika, black pepper, and red pepper flakes.

6. Bring the soup to a gentle boil over medium heat and cook for 5 minutes, or until the soup has thickened. Stir in the meatballs and peas, reduce the heat to low, and cover. Cook for 5 minutes.

7. Add the sour cream, stir, add the noodles, and mix in. Taste and season with additional salt and black pepper, if needed. Ladle into bowls and serve.

VARIATIONS

You can use a combination of beef and pork for the meatballs.

Cheesy Mac and Chicken Soup

Yield: Serves 4–6 | Prep Time: 15 minutes | Cook Time: 20–25 minutes

A friend of mine makes a recipe just like this for her daughter, and she absolutely loves it. So I decided to make a grown-up version. The paprika and Gouda cheese give the dish enough sophistication that it tastes like a dish from a fancy restaurant.

INGREDIENTS

2 cups dried elbow macaroni

3 tablespoons unsalted butter

3 tablespoons all-purpose flour

2 cups half-and-half

2 cups chicken broth

1 (10.75-ounce) can condensed cheddar cheese soup

½ teaspoon dry mustard

½ teaspoon garlic powder

½ teaspoon onion powder

½ teaspoon smoked paprika

½ teaspoon kosher salt

1 cup shredded sharp cheddar cheese

½ cup shredded smoked Gouda cheese

2 cups shredded cooked chicken (see Note)

8 bacon slices, cooked and crumbled

DIRECTIONS

1. Bring a large pot of water to a boil. Add the macaroni and cook until al dente according to the package instructions. Drain and set aside.

2. In a large pot, melt the butter over medium heat. Add the flour and whisk until combined. Cook, stirring, for 3 minutes, being careful not to brown the flour.

3. Gradually add in the half-and-half and broth, whisking until combined.

4. Add the cheddar cheese soup, mustard, garlic powder, onion powder, paprika, and salt.

5. Bring to a boil, then reduce the heat to low and simmer until thickened, 5 to 8 minutes.

6. Stir in the cheddar and Gouda cheeses until melted, about 3 minutes.

7. Add the chicken, macaroni, and half the bacon. Stir to combine and cook until the chicken is heated through.

8. If the soup is too thick, add additional broth or half-and-half to thin it to the desired consistency.

9. Ladle into bowls, top with the remaining bacon, and serve.

NOTE

To cook the chicken, place 2 medium boneless, skinless chicken breasts on a baking sheet and bake at 350°F for 30 minutes. Shred.

Chicken Noodle Soup

Yield: Serves 6–8 | Prep Time: 10 minutes | Cook Time: 30 minutes

There's no soup that takes me back to my childhood faster than Chicken Noodle Soup. This version includes onion, carrots, and celery, making it extra wholesome. Even as an adult, I find the egg noodles are as slurp-worthy as ever.

INGREDIENTS

2 tablespoons olive oil

3 pounds boneless, skinless chicken breasts, cut into 1-inch cubes

Kosher salt and freshly ground black pepper

1 onion, diced

3 carrots, cut into matchsticks

2 celery stalks, diced

2 garlic cloves, minced

8 cups low-sodium chicken broth

2 bay leaves

12 ounces extra-wide egg noodles

DIRECTIONS

1. In a large pot, heat the olive oil over medium heat. Add the chicken and season with salt and pepper. Stir and cook just until the chicken begins to color.

2. Add the onion, carrots, celery, garlic, broth, and bay leaves. Simmer until the vegetables are tender, 10 to 15 minutes.

3. Add the egg noodles and simmer until the noodles are cooked, according to the package instructions.

4. Turn off the heat and let rest for 5 minutes. Remove the bay leaves.

5. Ladle into bowls and serve.

Lemon Chicken Orzo Soup

Yield: Serves 6 | Prep Time: 10 minutes | Cook Time: 30 minutes

While orzo looks a lot like rice, it's actually a type of pasta. It contains more protein than a similar amount of brown rice, and like other pastas, it produces a resistant starch, which is an important source of fiber. The burst of lemon flavor makes this an ideal light soup for spring.

INGREDIENTS

2 tablespoons olive oil

1 pound boneless, skinless chicken breast, cut into 1-inch cubes

Kosher salt and freshly ground black pepper

3 garlic cloves, minced

1 onion, diced

3 carrots, sliced

2 celery stalks, diced

Leaves from 1 sprig fresh rosemary, chopped, plus additional sprigs for garnish

2 bay leaves

6 cups low-sodium chicken broth

¾ cup uncooked orzo pasta

Juice of 1 lemon

Lemon wheels, for garnish

DIRECTIONS

1. In a large pot, heat the olive oil over medium heat. Season the chicken with salt and pepper. Add the chicken to the pot and cook until lightly golden, 2 to 3 minutes per side.

2. Add the garlic, onion, carrots, celery, rosemary, and bay leaves. Cook, stirring occasionally, until the vegetables are tender, 3 to 4 minutes.

3. Add the broth, increase the heat to high, and bring to a boil. Stir in the orzo. Reduce the heat to low and simmer until the orzo is tender, 10 to 12 minutes. Stir in the lemon juice.

4. Remove the bay leaves.

5. Ladle into bowls, garnish with lemon wheels and rosemary, and serve immediately.

Chicken Parmesan Soup

Yield: Serves 4 | Prep Time: 15 minutes | Cook Time: 30 minutes

When I'm looking to do something a little creative in the kitchen, I try to think of how I can turn my favorite foods into something else. Can I make a bite-size pizza appetizer? What about a breakfast version of a classic pie? By transforming chicken Parm into soup form, I can enjoy that zing of Italian flavor while ladling something new!

INGREDIENTS

2 tablespoons olive oil

1 onion, diced

1 red bell pepper, seeded and diced

3 garlic cloves, minced

1 (15-ounce) can fire-roasted diced tomatoes

3 tablespoons tomato paste

1 teaspoon red pepper flakes

1 teaspoon Italian seasoning

5 cups chicken broth

8 ounces uncooked penne pasta

1 pound boneless, skinless chicken breasts, cooked and shredded (see Note)

½ teaspoon kosher salt

¼ teaspoon freshly ground black pepper

1½ cups shredded Parmesan cheese, plus extra for garnish

1 cup shredded mozzarella cheese

Fresh basil, for garnish

DIRECTIONS

1. In a large pot, heat the olive oil over medium-high heat. Add the onion and bell pepper and cook, stirring, for 5 to 6 minutes. Add the garlic and cook for another minute.

2. Add the tomatoes, tomato paste, red pepper flakes, Italian seasoning, and broth. Reduce the heat to low, bring to a simmer, and cook for 8 minutes.

3. Add the pasta and cooked chicken and cook for 8 to 10 minutes.

4. Season with the salt and black pepper.

5. Add the Parmesan and mozzarella cheeses and cook until melted, 3 to 4 minutes.

6. Ladle into bowls and serve, garnished with Parmesan cheese and basil.

NOTE

To cook the chicken, place the chicken breasts on a baking sheet and bake at 350°F for 30 minutes.

Miso Ramen Soup

Yield: Serves 2 | Prep Time: 15 minutes | Cook Time: 15–20 minutes

This particular ramen recipe is similar to a fancied-up version of microwaved ramen, giving the dorm room favorite a homemade touch. The saltiness of the noodles adds plenty of flavor to the dish, which is why you don't need a ton of spices to give it a bit of oomph.

INGREDIENTS

1 (4-ounce) package ramen noodles, seasoning packet discarded

6 shiitake mushrooms, sliced

1 hot chile, thinly sliced

3 baby bok choy, sliced

6 green onions, sliced

2 tablespoons red miso paste

1–2 teaspoons grated fresh ginger

2 tablespoons soy sauce

¾ cup frozen corn kernels, thawed, for garnish

½ red bell pepper, finely chopped, for garnish

1 boneless, skinless chicken breast, cooked and sliced, for garnish (see Note)

2 hard-boiled eggs, halved lengthwise, for garnish

Sesame oil, for serving

Sesame seeds, for garnish

DIRECTIONS

1. Bring a medium pot of water to a boil. Add the ramen and cook for 4 minutes, drain, and divide the noodles between large soup bowls.

2. In a large pot, bring 4 cups water to a simmer over medium heat. Add the mushrooms and hot chile.

3. Add the bok choy and green onions and cook just until they're bright green, 2 to 4 minutes.

4. Take off the heat and stir in the miso paste, ginger, and soy sauce.

5. Pour the broth over the noodles in each bowl.

6. Garnish with the corn, bell pepper, chicken, and egg halves. Drizzle with sesame oil and sprinkle with some sesame seeds. Serve.

NOTE

To cook the chicken, place chicken breasts on a baking sheet and bake at 350°F for 30 minutes.

Pasta e Fagioli Soup

Yield: Serves 8 | Prep Time: 10 minutes | Cook Time: 1½ hours

When I was growing up, I used to think this dish sounded so regal and fancy, but then I learned *pasta e fagioli* just means "pasta and beans" in Italian! Ditalini pasta works well in soups because the noodles are tiny enough to fit on a spoon, making the perfect bite, while the addition of ground beef makes the dish even heartier.

INGREDIENTS

1 pound lean ground beef

Kosher salt and freshly ground black pepper

1 cup diced onion

2 garlic cloves, minced

1 cup shredded carrot

1 cup chopped celery

1 tablespoon chopped fresh rosemary

½ cup red wine, such as Merlot or Cabernet (optional)

2 tablespoons tomato paste

1 (15-ounce) can diced tomatoes

1 (15-ounce) can tomato sauce

1 (15-ounce) can low-sodium chicken broth

1 (15-ounce) can red kidney beans, undrained

1 (15-ounce) can cannellini beans, undrained

1 teaspoon dried basil

½ teaspoon dried thyme

1 bay leaf

8 ounces uncooked ditalini pasta

Hot sauce, for serving

DIRECTIONS

1. In a large pot, brown the ground beef over medium-high heat until no longer pink, seasoning with salt and pepper. Add the onion, garlic, carrot, celery, and rosemary and cook, stirring occasionally, for 10 minutes.

2. Add the wine (if using) and the tomato paste to the pan. Stir to combine. Cook until the wine has reduced, about 5 minutes.

3. Add the diced tomatoes, tomato sauce, broth, kidney beans, cannellini beans, basil, thyme, and bay leaf. Stir well to combine.

4. Reduce the heat to low and simmer, stirring occasionally, for 1 hour.

5. Meanwhile, bring a large pot of water to a boil. Add the ditalini pasta and cook until al dente according to the package instructions. Drain and set aside.

6. When the soup is ready, remove from the heat and stir in the pasta. Remove the bay leaf, taste, and adjust the seasoning as needed.

7. Ladle into bowls and serve with hot sauce for passing at the table.

Lasagna Soup

Yield: Serves 4–5 | Prep Time: 15 minutes | Cook Time: 35–40 minutes

Whenever I make lasagna, I never use up the entire box of noodles. I put the half box back in my pantry where it seems to taunt me when I reach in to grab something else. I finally had to take action and make something new and interesting with what was left, serving as the inspiration for this dish! You can substitute other leftover pasta you have lying around if you wish.

INGREDIENTS

2 tablespoons olive oil

1 pound bulk Italian sausage

2 cups chopped onions

4 garlic cloves, minced

4 cups chicken broth

1 (28-ounce) can Italian plum tomatoes, crushed by hand

3 tablespoons tomato paste

1 teaspoon dried basil

1 teaspoon dried oregano

½ teaspoon crushed dried rosemary

1 teaspoon Italian seasoning

¼ teaspoon red pepper flakes

1 teaspoon sugar

2 tablespoons chopped fresh parsley

1 teaspoon kosher salt

1 teaspoon freshly ground black pepper

8 lasagna noodles, broken into bite-size pieces

1¼ cups shredded mozzarella cheese

½ cup grated Parmesan cheese

8 ounces ricotta cheese

Fresh basil leaves, for garnish

DIRECTIONS

1. In a large pot, heat 1 tablespoon of the olive oil over medium-high heat. Add the sausage to the pot and cook, breaking it up with a wooden spoon as it cooks, until browned, about 6 minutes. Transfer the sausage to a paper towel–lined plate to drain. Set aside.

2. Add the remaining 1 tablespoon olive oil to the pot. Add the onions and cook until tender, 3 to 4 minutes. Add the garlic and cook for another minute.

3. Add the broth, tomatoes, tomato paste, basil, oregano, rosemary, Italian seasoning, red pepper flakes, sugar, parsley, salt, black pepper, and cooked sausage.

4. Bring to a boil, reduce the heat to low, and simmer for 20 minutes.

5. Meanwhile, bring a large pot of water to a boil. Add the lasagna noodles and cook until al dente. Drain, reserving ½ cup of the pasta cooking water, and set aside.

6. Add the noodles and reserved pasta water to the soup.

7. In a small bowl, combine the mozzarella, Parmesan, and ricotta cheeses.

8. Ladle the soup into bowls, dollop with the cheese mixture, garnish with some fresh basil, and serve.

4

Vegetarian Soups

Soup is one of my favorite ways to sneak in some extra veggies. My husband is a dessert-eating machine, gobbling down one sugary treat after another. And while I admire his tenacity, I know that I have to find ways to sneak a few healthier ingredients into our dinner to balance everything out. He loves the Pumpkin Soup (page 139) for its sweet kick, and when I serve the Caramelized Onion Roasted Garlic Bisque (page 143), he barely has room for dessert. Soup is my secret healthy weapon, and I wield it with pride.

Matzo Ball Soup

Yield: Serves 4–6 | Prep Time: 25 minutes | Cook Time: 40–50 minutes

If you've never had matzo balls before, you're in for a treat. They have the fluffy, doughy texture of a dumpling, and since they're steamed in the broth, they soak up all the delicious flavors of the soup in each bite.

INGREDIENTS

Soup

1 tablespoon olive oil

1 large shallot, diced

1 (16-ounce) package baby carrots, cut into rounds

5 celery stalks, diced

3 garlic cloves, minced

2 cups vegetable broth

¼ teaspoon kosher salt

¼ teaspoon freshly ground black pepper

4 sprigs fresh parsley

2 sprigs fresh thyme

Matzo Balls

2 large eggs

2 tablespoons olive oil

1 (4.5-ounce) package matzo ball & soup mix

2 quarts vegetable broth

½ seasoning packet from the matzo ball & soup mix

½ teaspoon herbes de Provence

¼ teaspoon ground cumin

¼ teaspoon garlic powder

¼ teaspoon kosher salt

¼ teaspoon freshly ground black pepper

DIRECTIONS

1. *For the soup:* In a large pot, heat the olive oil over medium-high heat. Add the shallot, carrots, and celery and cook until tender, about 5 minutes. Add the garlic and cook for another minute.

2. Add the broth, salt, pepper, parsley, and thyme and simmer for 15 to 20 minutes.

3. *For the matzo balls:* In a medium bowl, whisk together the eggs and olive oil. Mix the matzo ball & soup mix into the eggs and olive oil and blend well. Refrigerate for 15 minutes.

4. In a medium pot, combine the broth and the seasoning from the matzo ball & soup mix. Bring to a boil over medium-high heat.

5. Remove the matzo ball dough from the fridge. Gently roll (do not pack) the dough into 10 balls about the size of a walnut.

6. Add the matzo balls to the boiling broth, reduce the heat, cover, and simmer for 20 minutes.

7. Gently spoon the matzo balls and their cooking liquid into the pot with the vegetables and broth.

8. Add the herbes de Provence, cumin, garlic powder, salt, and pepper. Taste and adjust the seasonings, if needed.

9. Ladle into bowls and serve.

Borscht

Yield: Serves 8 | Prep Time: 15 minutes | Cook Time: 30 minutes

Beets are a staple of eastern European diets, primarily because they can withstand the harsh, cold climates. I used jarred beets in this traditional Ukrainian recipe, but if beets are in season, feel free to use fresh ones!

INGREDIENTS

2 tablespoons olive oil

1 red onion, chopped

2 carrots, finely grated

½ leek, sliced and rinsed well

8 cups vegetable broth

1 small potato, peeled and cubed

2 cups jarred beets, cut into ½-inch cubes

2 cups thickly sliced red cabbage

1–2 teaspoons balsamic vinegar

Kosher salt and freshly ground black pepper

Sour cream, for garnish

Chopped fresh dill, for garnish

DIRECTIONS

1. In a large pot, heat the olive oil over medium-high heat. Add the onion and cook for 3 to 4 minutes, until it begins to soften.

2. Add the carrots and leek. Stir in the broth, potato, and beets. Cook for 10 minutes.

3. Add the cabbage and cook for 15 minutes.

4. Stir in the vinegar, salt, and pepper.

5. Ladle the soup into bowls. Garnish the soup with a dollop of sour cream and some dill. Serve.

Japanese Clear Onion Soup

Yield: Serves 4 | Prep Time: 10 minutes | Cook Time: 30 minutes

This veggie-filled broth soup is an easy pick-me-up on days when you're feeling a little down in the dumps. The mushrooms and onions are particularly prominent against the delightfully bitter broth. It's a thinner soup, making it perfect for a light lunch.

INGREDIENTS

2 tablespoons olive oil

2 onions, diced

2 carrots, diced

2 celery stalks, diced

2 garlic cloves, minced

½ teaspoon grated fresh ginger

6 cups vegetable broth

Sea salt and freshly ground black pepper

½ cup sliced cremini mushrooms

2 green onions, sliced

Soy sauce, for serving

Sriracha sauce, for serving

DIRECTIONS

1. In a medium pot, heat the olive oil over medium-high heat. Add the onions and cook until light brown, about 5 minutes.

2. Add the carrots, celery, garlic, and ginger. Stir in the broth. Bring to a boil, reduce the heat to low, and simmer for about 30 minutes.

3. Add the salt and pepper. Remove from the heat.

4. Strain the broth, reserving the vegetables to eat on the side.

5. Add the mushrooms and green onions to the broth.

6. Ladle into bowls. Season with soy sauce and Sriracha and serve.

Mulligatawny Soup

Yield: Serves 6 | Prep Time: 20 minutes | Cook Time: 40 minutes

Mulligatawny Soup is an English dish with roots in Indian cuisine that is oh-so-creamy and sweet. My favorite part is the mild crunch of apples, which is quite a unique addition to a soup.

INGREDIENTS

¼ cup olive oil

1 onion, chopped

1 carrot, diced

2 celery stalks, diced

1 small sweet potato, peeled and diced

3 garlic cloves, minced

2 teaspoons minced fresh ginger

2 small apples, peeled, cored, and diced

1 large tomato, diced

1 tablespoon curry powder

1 teaspoon ground cumin

½ teaspoon smoked paprika

½ teaspoon ground cinnamon

½ teaspoon ground turmeric

¼ teaspoon ground cardamom

¼ teaspoon freshly ground black pepper

½ teaspoon dried thyme

½ cup dried red or green lentils

3 cups vegetable broth

⅔ cup canned unsweetened coconut milk

Sea salt and freshly ground black pepper

Cashews, for garnish

Naan bread, for serving

DIRECTIONS

1. In a large pot, heat the olive oil over medium-high heat. Add the onion, carrot, celery, and sweet potato. Cook for 4 to 5 minutes, until the onion begins to soften.

2. Add the garlic, ginger, apples, and tomato. Cook for 3 to 4 minutes.

3. Add the curry powder, cumin, paprika, cinnamon, turmeric, cardamom, pepper, and thyme and mix well to combine.

4. Add the lentils and broth. Bring to a boil, then reduce the heat to medium-low and simmer for 30 minutes

5. Using a blender or an immersion blender, puree about three-quarters of the soup. Leave the rest of the soup chunky.

6. Return the pureed soup to the pot with the rest of the soup, if necessary.

7. Stir in the coconut milk. Season with salt and pepper.

8. Ladle the soup into bowls. Garnish with cashews and serve with naan bread.

Old-Fashioned Potato Soup

Yield: Serves 6 | Prep Time: 20 minutes | Cook Time: 1 hour

One of my husband's aunts gave me this recipe soon after we got engaged because it was one of Alex's favorite dishes growing up. When I asked her where it came from, she laughed and said that it'd just been in the family for years but she couldn't place its origin. The addition of flour makes the broth nice and thick, just the way I like it.

INGREDIENTS

4 tablespoons (½ stick) unsalted butter

1 small onion, diced

2 celery stalks, chopped

2 pounds potatoes, cut into large dice

½ pound baby carrots, chopped

Kosher salt and freshly ground black pepper

2 tablespoons all-purpose flour

2 cups vegetable broth

3 cups whole milk

¼ cup chopped fresh parsley

DIRECTIONS

1. In a large pot, melt the butter over medium heat. Add the onion and celery and cook until the onion is translucent and the celery begins to soften.

2. Add the potatoes and carrots to the pot. Season with salt and pepper. Stir in the flour and cook for 1 to 2 minutes. Add the broth and bring to a boil. Reduce the heat to low and simmer gently until the potatoes are tender, about 45 minutes.

3. Remove from the heat and stir in the milk and parsley. Cook until the soup begins to bubble again. Remove from the heat.

4. Ladle into bowls and serve.

French Onion Soup

Yield: Serves 4 | Prep Time: 15 minutes | Cook Time: 45 minutes

There's something about the melty, cheesy bread on top of French onion soup that speaks to my food-loving soul. You might want a few extra slices of cheesy baguette on hand to get double the cheesiness.

INGREDIENTS

4 tablespoons (½ stick) unsalted butter

4 large onions, very thinly sliced

3 garlic cloves, minced

4 sprigs fresh thyme

1 bay leaf

1 cup red wine

5 cups vegetable broth

Freshly ground black pepper

4 thick slices French baguette, plus more if desired

½ cup shredded Swiss cheese, plus more if desired

DIRECTIONS

1. In a large pot, melt the butter over medium heat. Add the onions and stir to combine. Cook, stirring occasionally, for 25 to 30 minutes, until the onions are a dark golden color; do not let them burn.

2. Add the garlic, fresh thyme, and bay leaf to the pot. Stir in the wine and cook until the liquid has reduced by half. Add the broth and pepper. Bring to a boil and reduce the heat to low. Simmer for 10 minutes.

3. Meanwhile, preheat the broiler.

4. Place the baguette slices on a baking sheet and top each slice with Swiss cheese. Place under the broiler and broil, watching carefully, until the cheese has melted and the top is lightly golden brown.

5. Remove the bay leaf and thyme sprigs from the soup.

6. Ladle the soup into crocks. Float a slice of toasted cheesy bread over each bowl and serve immediately.

Creamy Roasted Tomato-Basil Soup

Yield: Serves 4 | Prep Time: 15 minutes | Cook Time: 15 minutes

Tomato soup and grilled cheese go hand in hand. When I was a kid, I loved dunking the corner of my sandwich into the soup until there was nothing left. This homemade version of tomato soup is especially good for dunking because the garlic adds even more flavor.

INGREDIENTS

2 tablespoons olive oil

4 garlic cloves, minced

1 large onion, diced

2 (28-ounce) cans San Marzano plum tomatoes

1 cup vegetable broth

1 tablespoon sugar

¼ cup heavy cream

¼ cup fresh basil leaves, chopped, plus additional whole leaves for garnish

1 tablespoon fresh oregano leaves

Kosher salt and freshly ground black pepper

DIRECTIONS

1. In a large pot, heat the olive oil over medium heat. Add the garlic and onion and cook, stirring, until the onions have softened, about 5 minutes.

2. Add the tomatoes, broth, and sugar. Bring to a boil, reduce the heat to low, and simmer for about 10 minutes.

3. Remove from the heat and add the cream, basil, and oregano.

4. Using an immersion blender, puree the soup directly in the pot until there are no large pieces of tomato left. Taste and season with salt and pepper.

5. Ladle into bowls and serve, garnished with basil leaves.

Vegan Asparagus Soup

Yield: Serves 6 | Prep Time: 15 minutes | Cook Time: 20 minutes

The use of coconut milk and coconut oil makes this an even sweeter dish than traditional cream- or milk-based soups. Whenever I'm on a health kick, I refer back to this recipe to keep myself on track with my nutrition goals. The coconut milk adds a creamy texture that pairs well against the sharp crunch of the asparagus.

INGREDIENTS

1 tablespoon coconut oil

2 shallots, chopped

3 garlic cloves, minced

1½ pounds asparagus, ends snapped, cut into ½-inch pieces, plus more for garnish, if desired

1 tablespoon garam masala

1 teaspoon curry powder

1 teaspoon ground turmeric

2 cups vegetable broth

1 (15-ounce) can coconut milk

Juice of ½ lemon

¼ cup slivered almonds, for garnish

DIRECTIONS

1. In a large pot, heat the coconut oil over medium heat. Add the shallots and cook for 5 minutes.

2. Add the garlic and cook for 1 minute.

3. Stir in the asparagus and cook for 5 minutes.

4. Add the garam masala, curry powder, and turmeric, stir, and cook for 1 minute more.

5. Add the broth, stir, then add the coconut milk. Simmer for 5 to 10 minutes. Add the lemon juice.

6. Using a blender or immersion blender, puree the soup until it is completely smooth.

7. Ladle into bowls, top with slivered almonds and extra asparagus stalks, if desired, and serve.

Extra Creamy Mushroom Soup

Yield: Serves 4 | Prep Time: 5 minutes | Cook Time: 30 minutes

The heavy cream makes this soup rich and creamy, while the cremini mushrooms add an earthiness that tastes just right.

INGREDIENTS

3 tablespoons unsalted butter

1 onion, finely diced

1 pound cremini mushrooms, sliced

2 garlic cloves, finely minced

Kosher salt and freshly ground black pepper

3 tablespoons all-purpose flour

3 cups vegetable broth

1½ cups heavy cream

1 tablespoon Worcestershire sauce

Fresh thyme, for garnish

DIRECTIONS

1. In a large pot, melt the butter over medium heat. Add the onion, mushrooms, and garlic. Cook, stirring, until tender, about 5 minutes. Season with salt and pepper.

2. Add the flour and cook, stirring continuously, for 2 to 3 minutes. Gradually add the broth and bring to a boil, then reduce the heat to low and simmer, stirring occasionally, for 10 minutes.

3. Slowly stir in the cream and Worcestershire sauce and simmer for 5 minutes more, or until thickened.

4. Serve immediately, garnished with fresh thyme.

Potato-Leek Soup

Yield: Serves 4 | Prep Time: 10 minutes | Cook Time: 30–40 minutes

I like to think of leeks as the onion's mild-mannered cousin. They add flavor and presence to a dish, but they rarely overpower it.

INGREDIENTS

2 tablespoons olive oil

1 onion, diced

1 large leek, chopped and rinsed well

5 large Yukon Gold potatoes, diced

5 cups low-sodium vegetable broth

1 bay leaf

Kosher salt and freshly ground black pepper

2 cups half-and-half

Fried leek rings, for garnish (optional; see Note)

DIRECTIONS

1. In a large pot, heat the olive oil over medium-high heat. Add the onion and leek and cook, stirring, until softened, about 6 minutes. Add the potatoes, broth, bay leaf, salt, and pepper. Bring to a boil, reduce the heat to low, and simmer for 20 to 30 minutes, until the potatoes are tender.

2. Remove from the heat and add the half-and-half. Remove the bay leaf.

3. Using an immersion blender, puree the mixture directly in the pot to the desired consistency. The soup will thicken as it's pureed.

4. Ladle into bowls and serve garnished with fried leek rings, if desired.

NOTE

To make the fried leek rings: Carefully slice only the white part of 1 leek into ¼-inch-thick rings. Separate the rings and float them in a bowl of cold water to rinse any dirt away. Remove the rings from the water, leaving the dirt in the bowl, and soak the rings in ½ cup buttermilk. Meanwhile, heat 1 inch of olive oil in a heavy-bottomed saucepan over medium-high heat until the oil reaches 300°F. Remove the rings from the buttermilk and dredge in ½ cup biscuit baking mix. Transfer carefully to the hot oil and fry for 3 to 4 minutes, or until lightly golden brown. Transfer to a paper towel–lined baking sheet and sprinkle with kosher salt.

Pumpkin Soup

Yield: Serves 4–6 | Prep Time: 15 minutes | Cook Time: 30 minutes

I was looking through my cabinets one day and realized I had a couple extra cans of pumpkin left over from a pie I never wound up making. Instead of letting them sit around, I decided to throw together a homemade pumpkin soup! The canned pumpkin makes this dish possible any time of the year.

INGREDIENTS

1 tablespoon olive oil

3 shallots, diced

2 garlic cloves, smashed

2 teaspoons minced fresh ginger

1 tablespoon curry powder

2 teaspoons ground cumin

2 teaspoons ground coriander

¼ teaspoon ground cinnamon

1 teaspoon kosher salt

4 cups vegetable broth

2 (15-ounce) cans pure pumpkin puree

½ cup heavy cream

Crème fraîche, for serving

Fresh sage leaves, for serving

DIRECTIONS

1. In a large pot, heat the olive oil over medium-high heat. Add the shallots, garlic, and ginger and cook for 4 to 5 minutes.

2. Add the curry, cumin, coriander, cinnamon, and salt. Cook for 2 minutes.

3. Add the broth and pumpkin puree. Bring to a boil, then reduce the heat to low and simmer for 15 to 20 minutes.

4. Using an immersion blender or blender, puree the soup. If the soup is too thick, add more broth to thin it to the desired consistency.

5. Stir in the cream.

6. Ladle into bowls, top with a dollop of crème fraîche and sage leaves, and serve.

Carrot-Ginger Soup

Yield: Serves 4–6 | Prep Time: 20 minutes | Cook Time: 55–65 minutes

Allowing the carrots to roast and caramelize in the oven brings their sweet taste to the forefront. The hint of roasted garlic adds a delicate nutty flavor that makes it especially fitting for fall and winter.

INGREDIENTS

5 tablespoons olive oil

1 head garlic

3 pounds carrots

½ teaspoon kosher salt

¼ teaspoon freshly ground black pepper

1 teaspoon grated fresh ginger

5½ cups vegetable broth

1 teaspoon ground coriander

1 teaspoon ground allspice

2 teaspoons minced fresh thyme

1½ cups heavy cream

Fresh mint leaves, for garnish

DIRECTIONS

1. Preheat the oven to 425°F. Lightly oil a baking sheet with 2 tablespoons of the olive oil.

2. Remove the papery outer skin from the garlic head, leaving the cloves intact. Cut ¼ inch off the top of the head of the garlic, exposing the cloves, and drizzle the garlic with 1 tablespoon of the olive oil. Wrap the head in foil.

3. Put the carrots in a bowl, season with salt and pepper, and drizzle with the remaining 2 tablespoons olive oil. Spread the carrots on the prepared baking sheet. Set the foil-wrapped garlic on the baking sheet with the carrots.

4. Roast for 45 to 50 minutes, turning the carrots over halfway through roasting, until tender and caramelized. Remove from the oven and let cool slightly. Cut the carrots into chunks.

5. Unwrap the roasted garlic and squeeze the garlic cloves from the papery skins into a small bowl.

6. Combine the carrots, roasted garlic, ginger, and 3 cups of the broth in a food processor and puree until smooth.

7. Pour the carrot puree into a large pot. Add the remaining 2½ cups broth, the coriander, allspice, and thyme. Cook over medium heat until the soup just begins to bubble.

8. Reduce the heat to medium-low, stir in the cream, and heat for 3 to 4 minutes to warm through.

9. Ladle into bowls, garnish with mint leaves, and serve.

Caramelized Onion Roasted Garlic Bisque

Yield: Serves 6 | Prep Time: 20 minutes | Cook Time: 2 hours

While you could certainly enjoy this for dinner, I love making a batch and packing it up in a thermos to bring to work. It's not too messy, and it's easy to dunk a piece of crusty bread in if you have extra lying around the kitchen.

INGREDIENTS

1 head garlic

5 teaspoons olive oil

9 cups thinly sliced sweet onions

2½ cups sliced leeks, rinsed well

1 large shallot, sliced

1 teaspoon kosher salt

2 teaspoons minced fresh thyme

2 teaspoons chopped fresh sage

2 tablespoons all-purpose flour

4 cups vegetable broth

⅓ cup white wine

2 cups heavy cream

Fresh thyme leaves, for garnish

DIRECTIONS

1. Preheat the oven to 400°F.

2. Remove the papery outer skin from the garlic head, leaving the cloves intact. Cut ¼ inch off the top of the head of the garlic, exposing the cloves, and drizzle with 2 teaspoons of the olive oil. Wrap in foil. Roast for 45 minutes.

3. Let cool slightly. Gently squeeze the roasted garlic cloves out of the papery skins into a small bowl and set aside.

4. While the garlic roasts, in a large pot, heat the remaining 3 teaspoons olive oil over medium heat. Add the onions, leeks, and shallot and cook, stirring often, for 30 minutes.

5. Add ½ teaspoon of the salt, the thyme, and the sage. Cook, stirring often so the onions do not burn, for 30 minutes, until the onions are a dark golden color.

6. Stir in the flour and cook for 1 minute. Add the broth and wine and bring to a boil. Reduce the heat to low and simmer for 30 minutes.

7. Combine the roasted garlic, remaining ½ teaspoon salt, and the cooked onion mixture in a blender. Puree until smooth.

8. Pour the pureed onion mixture back into the pot and add the cream. Simmer over low heat for 8 to 10 minutes until heated.

9. Ladle into bowls, garnish with thyme leaves, and serve.

Vegetable Soup

Yield: Serves 6–7 | Prep Time: 20 minutes | Cook Time: 40–45 minutes

I like to think of this as my "farmers market soup." While I use carrots and celery here, I'll often change this recipe up to suit whatever happens to be in season (like adding broccoli in the winter or squash in the fall).

INGREDIENTS

3 tablespoons olive oil

2 leeks, white and light green parts only, chopped and rinsed well

2 cups chopped carrots

1½ cups chopped celery

4 garlic cloves, minced

4 cups vegetable broth

3 cups diced potatoes

1 (28-ounce) can diced tomatoes

⅓ cup chopped fresh parsley

1 tablespoon Worcestershire sauce

2 bay leaves

1 tablespoon chopped fresh thyme

½ teaspoon herbes de Provence

1 teaspoon kosher salt

½ teaspoon freshly ground black pepper

1 cup frozen chopped green beans

1 cup frozen corn kernels

DIRECTIONS

1. In a large pot, heat the olive oil over medium-high heat. Add the leeks, carrots, and celery and cook for 5 minutes. Add the garlic and cook for another minute.

2. Add the broth, potatoes, tomatoes, parsley, Worcestershire sauce, bay leaves, thyme, herbes de Provence, salt, and pepper. Bring to a boil. Add the green beans, reduce the heat to low, and simmer for 20 to 30 minutes, until the vegetables are tender.

3. Add the corn and cook for 5 minutes more.

4. Ladle into bowls and serve.

Throw-Together Tortellini Soup

Yield: Serves 6–8 | Prep Time: 5 minutes | Cook Time: 20 minutes

Tortellini is your new best friend if you're trying to pull together a home-cooked meal in a rush. Since they come prestuffed with other ingredients, most of the work is done for you. All you need to do is add a few other ingredients to the pot to create a full-fledged dinner.

INGREDIENTS

4–5 cups vegetable broth

2 (28-ounce) cans diced tomatoes

1 (20-ounce) bag frozen cheese tortellini

10 ounces baby spinach, chopped

1 tablespoon Italian seasoning

Kosher salt and freshly ground black pepper

Grated Parmesan cheese, for garnish

DIRECTIONS

1. In a large pot, combine 4 cups of the broth, the tomatoes, tortellini, spinach, and Italian seasoning. Bring to a boil over medium-high heat, then reduce the heat to low and simmer for 15 minutes.

2. Add more broth if needed. Season with a few pinches of salt and pepper.

3. Ladle into bowls, sprinkle with Parmesan, and serve.

Made-from-Scratch Minestrone Soup

Yield: Serves 6–8 | Prep Time: 15 minutes | Cook Time: 30 minutes

When I was growing up, there was a family-owned restaurant a few towns over that featured minestrone soup as the "Soup of the Day" every Monday. My brother and I loved going there on the Mondays we had off from school. The version here is a bit more grown-up, with the addition of dry red wine, which gives the soup an even richer taste.

INGREDIENTS

8 ounces uncooked mini pasta shells

2 tablespoons olive oil

½ onion, diced

8 ounces shredded carrots

2 celery stalks, chopped

3 garlic cloves, minced

1 cup dry red wine

1 tablespoon chopped fresh thyme

2 bay leaves

1 (15.5-ounce) can cannellini beans, drained and rinsed

1 (14.5-ounce) can diced tomatoes

4 cups vegetable broth, preferably low-sodium

Kosher salt and freshly ground black pepper

2 cups fresh spinach, cleaned well and chopped

1 small zucchini, chopped

DIRECTIONS

1. Bring a small pot of water to a boil. Add the pasta and cook until al dente. Drain and set aside.

2. In a large pot, heat the olive oil over medium-high heat. Add the onion, carrots, celery, and garlic. Cook, stirring, until the vegetables begin to soften, about 4 minutes.

3. Add the wine, scraping up any bits from the bottom of the pan. Bring to a boil to reduce the liquid. Add the thyme and bay leaves to the pot and stir well.

4. Add the beans, tomatoes, broth, salt, and pepper. Reduce the heat to medium-low and simmer for 20 minutes.

5. Add the spinach and zucchini and simmer for 5 minutes, until the vegetables soften.

6. Stir in the cooked pasta. Remove the bay leaves.

7. Ladle into bowls and serve.

Veggie Soba Noodle Soup

Yield: Serves 5 | Prep Time: 20 minutes | Cook Time: 20 minutes

Soba is a buckwheat noodle commonly used in Japanese cuisine. The slippery, smooth texture makes it the ideal slurping noodle; not to mention, the leftover soup tastes just as good cold as it does hot.

INGREDIENTS

1 tablespoon sesame oil

3 garlic cloves, minced

4 green onions, chopped

3 heads bok choy with leaves, chopped

2 celery stalks, chopped

4 ounces shiitake mushrooms, sliced

4 ounces cremini mushrooms, sliced

5 cups vegetable broth

2 cups water

2 cups fresh spinach, chopped

4–5 ounces uncooked soba noodles

3 tablespoons soy sauce

1 tablespoon rice vinegar

½ teaspoon Sriracha sauce

½ teaspoon kosher salt

¼ teaspoon freshly ground black pepper

3 tablespoons chopped fresh cilantro, plus more for garnish

1½ teaspoons minced fresh ginger

Juice of ½ lime

DIRECTIONS

1. In a large pot, heat the sesame oil over medium-high heat. Add the garlic and green onions and cook for 3 minutes.

2. Add the bok choy, celery, shiitake and cremini mushrooms, broth, and 2 cups water. Bring to a boil, cover, and cook for 8 minutes.

3. Add the spinach, noodles, soy sauce, vinegar, Sriracha, salt, pepper, cilantro, and ginger.

4. Boil until the noodles are cooked, about 4 minutes. Add the lime juice.

5. Ladle into bowls, garnish with cilantro, and serve.

5

Stews

Stews are popular if you're looking to save money at the grocery
store. Since the ingredients cook slowly, the meat has time to
moisten and tenderize, allowing even the toughest cuts of meat to shine.
And you don't need to sacrifice diversity when you make a stew.
You can try something as unique as West African Vegetable
Stew (page 160) or a family favorite like Slow Cooker
Creamy Chicken Stew (page 167).

1-Hour Turkey Stew

Yield: Serves 4 | Prep Time: 20 minutes | Cook Time: 35–40 minutes

When the weatherman warns of a possible snowstorm on the horizon, I'll run to the grocery store and stock up on everything I need to make my favorite stews, like this quick turkey stew. The addition of potatoes and a side of biscuits make this dish especially filling, fitting for even the most blustery days.

INGREDIENTS

1 tablespoon olive oil

3 celery stalks, cut into ½-inch pieces

1 onion, chopped

2 carrots, cut into ½-inch pieces

3 potatoes, peeled and cut into ½-inch pieces

4¾ cups chicken broth

½ teaspoon dried sage

½ teaspoon herbes de Provence

½ teaspoon kosher salt

½ teaspoon freshly ground black pepper

1 tablespoon Worcestershire sauce

2 tablespoons all-purpose flour

3 cups 1-inch pieces cooked turkey

1 cup cut frozen green beans

DIRECTIONS

1. In a large pot, heat the olive oil over high heat. Add the celery, onion, and carrots and cook for 5 minutes.

2. Add the potatoes, 4 cups of the broth, the sage, herbes de Provence, salt, pepper, and Worcestershire sauce.

3. Bring to a boil, reduce the heat to low, and cook for 18 to 20 minutes.

4. In a small bowl, mix the remaining ¾ cup broth with the flour and blend well. Pour the mixture into the soup and stir.

5. Add the turkey and green beans and cook for 8 to 10 minutes, until hot.

6. Ladle into bowls and serve.

Quick Beef Stew

Yield: Serves 4 | Prep Time: 15 minutes | Cook Time: 40 minutes

I remember visiting my grandma's house over winter break and asking her to make her famous beef stew. We'd wait for hours for it to simmer on the stovetop, my stomach rumbling the entire time. I think this 1-hour version is just as good as hers, but I don't have to wait quite as long to enjoy it!

INGREDIENTS

2 tablespoons olive oil

8 ounces cremini mushrooms, quartered

2 pounds boneless beef chuck roast, cut into 1-inch chunks

3 carrots, cut into 1-inch chunks

2 onions, cut into 1-inch wedges

3 potatoes, peeled and cut into 1-inch chunks

2 teaspoons kosher salt

1 teaspoon freshly ground black pepper

4 cups beef broth

½ cup red wine

1 tablespoon minced fresh thyme

1 tablespoon Worcestershire sauce

¼ cup all-purpose flour

DIRECTIONS

1. In a large pot, heat ½ tablespoon of the olive oil over medium heat. Add the mushrooms and cook until they begin to brown, about 4 minutes. Transfer to a bowl and set aside.

2. Raise the heat to medium-high and heat 1 tablespoon of the olive oil. Add the beef chunks and cook until browned on all sides, about 8 minutes. Transfer to a plate.

3. Reduce the heat to medium and heat the remaining ½ tablespoon olive oil. Add the carrots and cook for 4 minutes. Add the onions and cook for 5 minutes more. Add the potatoes, salt, pepper, 3 cups of the broth, the wine, thyme, and Worcestershire sauce. Return the mushrooms and beef to the pot. Bring to a boil, reduce the heat to low, and simmer for 10 to 15 minutes.

4. In a small bowl, mix the remaining 1 cup broth with the flour. Add the mixture to the pot and cook for 5 minutes, until the stew has thickened.

5. Ladle into bowls and serve.

Country Chicken Stew

Yield: Serves 4 | Prep Time: 15 minutes | Cook Time: 35–45 minutes

When I think of country cooking, I think of chicken and potatoes stewing on the stovetop with vegetables from the garden thrown in for added flavor. This recipe is inspired by that aesthetic with a combination of chicken, carrots, bacon, potatoes, and spices for a down-home feel.

INGREDIENTS

2 bacon slices, diced

1 onion, sliced

1 (10.75-ounce) can condensed cream of chicken soup

1 (10.75-ounce) soup can half-and-half

3 cups cubed, peeled potatoes

1 cup sliced carrots

1 teaspoon minced fresh thyme

½ teaspoon kosher salt

½ teaspoon freshly ground black pepper

1 cup cut frozen green beans or fresh green beans

½ pound boneless, skinless chicken, cooked and cut into 1-inch cubes (see Note)

2 tablespoons chopped fresh parsley

Biscuits, refrigerated or homemade, for serving

DIRECTIONS

1. In a large deep skillet, cook the bacon until crispy. Remove and place on paper towels to drain.

2. Add the onion to the skillet and cook for 4 to 5 minutes, until tender.

3. Stir in the cream of chicken soup, half-and-half, potatoes, carrots, thyme, salt, and pepper. Bring to a boil, then reduce the heat to low, cover, and simmer for 15 minutes.

4. Stir in the green beans, cover, and cook for 10 to 15 minutes more, until the vegetables are tender.

5. Add the cooked chicken, parsley, and bacon. Cook until the stew is hot, about 4 minutes.

6. Ladle into bowls and serve with warm biscuits.

NOTE

To cook the chicken, place the chicken breast on a baking sheet and bake at 350°F for 30 minutes.

West African Vegetable Stew

Yield: Serves 6 | Prep Time: 20 minutes | Cook Time: 45 minutes

My favorite part about this recipe is the sweet, nutty taste that accompanies a stew made with peanut butter and coconut milk. I like to serve it topped with a handful of rice to get a full, hearty meal.

INGREDIENTS

2 tablespoons olive oil

1 pound boneless, skinless chicken thighs, cubed

1 onion, quartered

2 zucchini, chopped

1 red bell pepper, large diced

4 ounces cremini mushrooms, sliced

5 baby red potatoes, quartered

1 (15-ounce) can fire-roasted diced tomatoes

Kosher salt and freshly ground black pepper

2 large garlic cloves, minced

¼ teaspoon cayenne pepper

1 (15-ounce) can chickpeas, drained and rinsed

½ cup creamy peanut butter

1 tablespoon tomato paste

1 teaspoon Sriracha sauce

1 teaspoon grated fresh ginger

½ cup coconut milk

2 cups water

¼ cup chopped fresh parsley, for garnish

Prepared white rice, for serving

DIRECTIONS

1. In a large pot, heat the olive oil over medium-high heat. Add the chicken and cook, stirring occasionally, until all sides are lightly golden but the chicken is not cooked through. Add the onion, zucchini, bell pepper, mushrooms, potatoes, diced tomatoes, salt, black pepper, garlic, and cayenne. Cook, stirring, for 8 minutes, until the onion is translucent and the vegetables are browning in spots.

2. Add the chickpeas, peanut butter, tomato paste, Sriracha, ginger, coconut milk, and 2 cups water. Reduce the heat to low, bring to a simmer, and cook, stirring occasionally, for 30 minutes, or until the sauce thickens and all the vegetables are tender.

3. Ladle into bowls, garnish with chopped parsley, and serve with a scoop of rice.

White Bean Chicken Stew

Yield: Serves 4–6 | Prep Time: 20 minutes | Cook Time: 1 hour

This rustic stew takes on a slightly smoky flavor with all that bacon. The real star of the show, though, are the chicken thighs. They are cheaper to buy at the grocery store than chicken breasts and are packed with even more flavor—plus, they stay moist.

INGREDIENTS

2 tablespoons olive oil

6 smoked bacon slices, chopped

2 tablespoons unsalted butter

1 onion, diced

1 carrot, sliced

1 zucchini, sliced

2 celery stalks, diced

1 (15-ounce) can small white beans, drained and rinsed

1 (15.5-ounce) can navy beans, drained and rinsed

5 garlic cloves, minced

2 teaspoons dried oregano

1 teaspoon sea salt

1 teaspoon freshly ground black pepper

4 cups chicken broth

2 (28-ounce) cans crushed tomatoes

4 boneless, skinless chicken thighs, cooked

DIRECTIONS

1. Heat a large Dutch oven or heavy-bottomed pot over medium-high heat.

2. Once the pot is hot, put in 1 tablespoon of the olive oil and the chopped bacon. Cook until the bacon is crispy, then remove with a slotted spoon and set aside.

3. Wipe out the pot and return it to medium-high heat. Put the remaining 1 tablespoon olive oil and the butter into the pot. Once the butter is melted and sizzling, add the onion, carrot, zucchini, and celery and cook until softened, about 5 minutes.

4. Add the bacon, white beans, navy beans, garlic, oregano, salt, and pepper. Stir to combine.

5. Add the broth, tomatoes, and chicken and stir. Partially cover the pot with a lid and gently simmer for 40 to 45 minutes.

6. Ladle into bowls and serve.

NOTES

To cook the chicken, place 4 medium boneless, skinless chicken thighs on a baking sheet and bake at 350°F for 30 minutes.

Cajun Chicken and Mushroom Stew

Yield: Serves 4 | Prep Time: 10 minutes | Cook Time: 1½ hours

I love using chicken thighs when I can in my cooking because the extra juices from the bird add so much extra flavor to the dish without needing to load it up with spices. The Worcestershire sauce and hot sauce topping give it an extra kick of flavor.

INGREDIENTS

4 tablespoons (½ stick) unsalted butter, melted

1 pound boneless, skinless chicken thighs, roughly chopped

Kosher salt and freshly ground black pepper

¼ cup all-purpose flour

1 onion, diced

2 celery stalks, chopped

1 red bell pepper, diced

1–2 garlic cloves, chopped

8 ounces cremini mushrooms, sliced

1 bay leaf

2 (15-ounce) cans low-sodium chicken broth

2 teaspoons Worcestershire sauce

Hot sauce, for serving

DIRECTIONS

1. In a Dutch oven, melt the butter over medium heat. Add the chicken and cook until browned. Season with salt and black pepper.

2. Stir in the flour and cook, stirring continuously, until the flour becomes a rich chocolate brown, about 10 minutes.

3. Add the onion, celery, bell pepper, garlic, mushrooms, and bay leaf and cook until the onion is translucent and the vegetables are softened.

4. Add the broth, stirring to remove any lumps.

5. Add the Worcestershire sauce, taste, and adjust the seasoning, if needed.

6. Cover and simmer for 1 hour.

7. Remove the bay leaf.

8. Ladle into bowls, and serve with hot sauce for passing at the table.

Slow Cooker Creamy Chicken Stew

Yield: Serves 4 | Prep Time: 5 minutes | Cook Time: 3–4 hours on High or 5–6 hours on Low

The secret to adding flavor to this chicken stew is in the ranch dressing mix. One packet contains a blend of spices like garlic powder, dry buttermilk, onion powder, and more that make the stew extra creamy.

INGREDIENTS

1 pound boneless, skinless chicken breasts, cubed

1 onion, diced

5 small red potatoes, quartered

1 cup baby carrots, chopped in half

2 celery stalks, diced

Kosher salt and freshly ground black pepper

1 tablespoon unsalted butter, melted

1 (10-ounce) can cream of chicken soup

½ cup whole milk

½ cup sour cream

1 (1-ounce) packet dry ranch dressing mix

1 teaspoon dried thyme

Fresh parsley, for garnish

DIRECTIONS

1. In a 6-quart slow cooker, combine the chicken breasts, onion, potatoes, carrots, and celery. Season with salt and pepper. Drizzle the melted butter over and stir to coat.

2. In a medium bowl, combine the soup, milk, sour cream, ranch dressing mix, and thyme. Pour the mixture into the slow cooker.

3. Cover and cook on High for 3 to 4 hours or on Low for 5 to 6 hours.

4. Ladle into bowls, garnish with parsley, and serve.

Leftover Turkey Stew

Yield: Serves 4–6 | Prep Time: 15 minutes | Cook Time: 25 minutes

I get into turkey kicks throughout the year, not just during Thanksgiving. I'll cook a full turkey for dinner and find ways to use the leftovers in all kinds of things: salads, sandwiches, and, of course, stews. If you want an even thicker stew, add more flour.

INGREDIENTS

2 tablespoons unsalted butter

1 onion, diced

2 celery stalks, diced

½ teaspoon kosher salt, plus more to taste

¼ cup all-purpose flour

6 yellow potatoes, diced

4 cups chicken broth

1½ cups half-and-half

1 tablespoon minced fresh thyme

½ teaspoon freshly ground black pepper, plus more to taste

2 pounds shredded or chopped leftover turkey meat

DIRECTIONS

1. In a large Dutch oven, melt the butter over medium-high heat. Add the onion and celery and season with the salt. Cook, stirring, for about 2 minutes, then stir in the flour and cook for 1 minute.

2. Add the potatoes, broth, half-and-half, thyme, and pepper. Bring to a boil, then reduce the heat to medium and cover. Simmer for about 15 minutes. Stir in the turkey and simmer for 5 minutes more. Taste and season with salt and pepper.

3. Ladle into bowls and serve.

Beef Barley Stew

Yield: Serves 8 | Prep Time: 15 minutes | Cook Time: 65–75 minutes

I'm a big fan of beef stew, but sometimes I want something a bit lighter. The broth isn't as thick in the recipe, but you still get plenty of meat and veggies to fill you up. The sliced mushrooms in particular are a soft contrast against the sturdier beef.

INGREDIENTS

2 tablespoons olive oil

1 pound beef stew meat, cut into ½-inch pieces

1 onion, chopped

½ pound sliced cremini mushrooms

3 carrots, diced

8 cups beef broth

1 (14.5-ounce) can fire-roasted diced tomatoes, with their juices

1 bay leaf

1 tablespoon minced fresh thyme

½ teaspoon herbes de Provence

½ teaspoon kosher salt

½ teaspoon freshly ground black pepper

1 cup frozen peas

¾ cup quick-cooking barley

DIRECTIONS

1. In a large pot, heat the olive oil over high heat. Add the beef, onion, mushrooms, and carrots and cook for 6 to 8 minutes, until the beef is browned.

2. Add the broth, tomatoes with their juices, bay leaf, thyme, herbes de Provence, salt, and pepper. Bring to a boil, then reduce the heat to low and simmer for 30 minutes.

3. Add the peas and barley. Cook for 15 to 20 minutes more, until the barley is tender.

4. Remove the bay leaf, ladle into bowls, and serve.

Ham Bone Stew

Yield: Serves 4 | Prep Time: 15 minutes | Cook Time: 1 hour 50 minutes

My mother-in-law refers to this as her "Christmas leftover stew." We both like to find new uses for leftovers after the holidays, and this Ham Bone Stew is the perfect solution.

INGREDIENTS

1 cup chopped onions

1 cup chopped carrots

½ cup chopped celery

2 garlic cloves, minced

1 ham bone

1 bay leaf

8 cups chicken broth

1 (15.5-ounce) can white beans, undrained

2 cups kale, stemmed, leaves chopped

1 teaspoon herbes de Provence

¼ teaspoon kosher salt

¼ teaspoon freshly ground black pepper

3 bacon slices, cooked and crumbled, for garnish

DIRECTIONS

1. In a large pot, combine the onions, carrots, celery, and garlic and cook for 3 to 4 minutes on medium-high heat.

2. Add the ham bone, bay leaf, and broth and bring to a boil.

3. Reduce the heat to low and simmer for 1 hour.

4. Remove the ham bone and the bay leaf.

5. Carefully transfer the broth to a blender and blend until smooth, then return to the pot. (Alternatively, puree the broth directly in the pot with an immersion blender.)

6. Return the ham bone to the pureed broth.

7. Add the beans and cook for 20 minutes more.

8. Add the kale and herbes de Provence and cook for 15 to 20 minutes more.

9. Remove the ham bone, take the meat off the bone, and add the meat to the stew.

10. Season with the salt and pepper.

11. Ladle into bowls and serve topped with the crumbled bacon.

Easy Kentucky Burgoo

Yield: Serves 6–8 | Prep Time: 30 minutes | Cook Time: 1 hour 45 minutes

Burgoo is a special kind of stew from Kentucky that has a few unique characteristics: the meat needs to be cooked on its own first before it's mixed with any veggies, several types of meat are used, and the meat is simmered slowly on the stovetop instead of getting cooked more quickly like in soups. I use a few shortcut ingredients to make it easier! Serve with a side of cornbread to complete the meal.

INGREDIENTS

2 tablespoons olive oil

1 pound boneless, skinless chicken thighs, cut into bite-size pieces

1 pound boneless, skinless chicken breasts, cut into bite-size pieces

½ pound boneless pork tenderloin, cut into bite-size pieces

1 pound beef top round, cut into ½-inch cubes

1 green bell pepper, seeded and chopped

1 onion, chopped

2 garlic cloves, chopped

6 cups beef broth

1 (6-ounce) can tomato paste

3 tablespoons Worcestershire sauce

¼ teaspoon cayenne pepper

1 (16-ounce) bag frozen corn kernels

1 (16-ounce) bag frozen lima beans

1–2 Yukon Gold potatoes, peeled and cubed

2 tablespoons hot sauce

DIRECTIONS

1. In a large pot, heat the olive oil over medium-high heat. Add the chicken thighs, chicken breasts, pork tenderloin, and beef. Cook, stirring occasionally, for 5 to 7 minutes, until the meat starts to brown.

2. Add the bell pepper, onion, and garlic and cook for 5 minutes more.

3. Add the broth, tomato paste, Worcestershire sauce, and cayenne. Bring to a boil, then reduce the heat to low, cover, and simmer for 1 hour.

4. Add the corn, lima beans, potatoes, and hot sauce. Cook over medium heat for 30 minutes, until thickened.

5. Ladle into bowls and serve.

Brazilian Fish Stew

Yield: Serves 4 | Prep Time: 20 minutes | Cook Time: 35–40 minutes

This traditional Brazilian dish is enriched by the addition of coconut oil and coconut milk, adding a creamy, tropical flavor to contrast against the spicy jalapeño. The garlic rice acts as a savory counterpart.

INGREDIENTS

Stew

2 tablespoons coconut oil

1 teaspoon olive oil

½ onion, chopped

1 red bell pepper, seeded and sliced

1 yellow bell pepper, seeded and sliced

1 jalapeño, chopped

3 garlic cloves, minced

1 teaspoon smoked paprika

¼ teaspoon cayenne pepper

½ pound cod, cut into 2-inch chunks

½ pound swordfish, cut into 2-inch chunks

½ pound medium raw shrimp, peeled and deveined

Kosher salt and freshly ground black pepper

2 cups vegetable broth

1 (13.5-ounce) can coconut milk

Zest of 1 lime

Rice

1 tablespoon olive oil

½ onion, finely chopped

1 garlic clove, minced

1 cup uncooked jasmine rice

2 cups vegetable broth

¼ teaspoon kosher salt

¼ teaspoon freshly ground black pepper

Lime wedges, for garnish

Green onions, sliced, for garnish

Chopped cilantro, for garnish

DIRECTIONS

1. *For the stew:* In a large pot, heat the coconut oil and olive oil over medium heat. Add the onion, bell peppers, and jalapeño and cook for 6 to 8 minutes, until the vegetables are softened.

2. Stir in the garlic, paprika, and cayenne and cook for 2 minutes more.

3. Season the cod, swordfish, and shrimp with salt and black pepper on both sides, then place over the vegetables. Pour the broth and coconut milk over the fish and vegetables.

4. Add the lime zest and a few pinches of salt and black pepper.

5. Cover and cook on medium-low heat for 25 to 30 minutes, until the fish and shrimp are cooked through and opaque.

6. *For the rice:* In a small saucepan, heat the olive oil over medium heat. Add the onion and garlic. Cook until the onion is caramelized, 5 minutes.

7. Add the rice and stir to coat. Add the broth, salt, and pepper. Bring to a boil, reduce the heat to low, cover, and simmer for about 20 minutes, until the rice is cooked.

8. Fluff the rice with a fork. Ladle the fish stew into bowls and serve with a side of rice. Garnish with lime wedges, green onions, and cilantro.

Crab Stew

Yield: Serves 4–6 | Prep Time: 15 minutes | Cook Time: 40 minutes

This dish is something I make when I want to treat myself but don't feel like going to a stuffy sit-down restaurant. Be sure you use a dry, crisp wine like a Pinot Grigio when making this to avoid adding unnecessary sweetness.

INGREDIENTS

½ cup (1 stick) unsalted butter

1 fennel bulb, thinly sliced

2 celery stalks, finely chopped

½ cup all-purpose flour

¼ cup dry white wine, such as Pinot Grigio

4 cups heavy cream

2 cups half-and-half

4 cups seafood stock

2 pounds crabmeat, shredded

Kosher salt and freshly ground black pepper

DIRECTIONS

1. In a large saucepan, melt the butter over medium heat. Add the fennel and celery and stir to combine. Cook until the vegetables are softened, about 5 minutes. Stir in the flour until it has been completely absorbed. Cook, stirring, for 8 to 10 minutes more. The mixture will begin to thicken and turn a light golden color.

2. Pour the wine into the pan, stirring vigorously to remove any lumps. Cook to reduce the wine by about half, 5 minutes more. Add the cream, half-and-half, and seafood stock. Simmer to thicken the stew, 8 minutes more.

3. Add the crabmeat to the stew, taste, and season with salt and pepper. Cook until the crabmeat is heated through.

4. Ladle into bowls and serve.

6

Chilis

Anytime my husband and I invite friends over to watch hockey, we
have a slow cooker full of chili waiting for everyone to dive into.
And when we tailgate before a football game, I pack a couple of
thermoses filled with freshly made chili to keep us warm against
the brisk cold. I don't know why sports and chili seem to go together
so well, but it's a combination I wouldn't want to do without.

White Chicken Chili

Yield: Serves 4–6 | Prep Time: 10 minutes | Cook Time: 30 minutes

Every time I make chili for a crowd, there's someone in the group who wants to knock it for being too spicy. This is the only chili I've been able to make that passes the spice test time and time again. While there are a couple of poblano peppers in the mix, they have a much milder taste, making it palatable even for those who don't like the heat!

INGREDIENTS

1 tablespoon olive oil

1 large onion, diced

2 poblano peppers, seeded and diced

5 garlic cloves, minced

¼ cup fresh cilantro, chopped

1 tablespoon ground cumin

1 teaspoon ground coriander

1 teaspoon Mexican-style chili powder

Kosher salt and freshly ground black pepper

2 (15.5-ounce) cans cannellini beans, drained and rinsed

4 cups diced cooked chicken (see Note)

4 cups low-sodium chicken broth

1 (5-ounce) can diced green chiles

Juice of 1 lime

DIRECTIONS

1. In a large pot, heat the olive oil over medium heat. Add the onion and poblanos and cook, stirring until softened, about 5 minutes.

2. Add the garlic and stir until fragrant.

3. Add the cilantro, cumin, coriander, chili powder, salt, and black pepper and cook for 2 minutes, until the spices are toasted and fragrant.

4. Add the beans, chicken, broth, green chiles, and lime juice. Bring to a boil, then reduce the heat to low. Simmer for 20 to 25 minutes.

5. Ladle into bowls and serve.

NOTE

To cook the chicken, place 4 medium boneless, skinless chicken breasts on a baking sheet and bake at 350°F for 30 minutes.

Classic Slow Cooker Chili

Yield: Serves 8–10 | Prep Time: 15 minutes | Cook Time: 8 hours

I've made many chili recipes in my day, and when it comes right down to it, simple and classic can be the best option. This version is a touch spicy without being overwhelming, while incorporating plenty of beans and veggies to give the dish variety.

INGREDIENTS

2 pounds lean ground beef

1 onion, chopped

1 green bell pepper, diced

4 garlic cloves, minced

3 tablespoons chili powder

2 teaspoons ground cumin

1 teaspoon dried oregano

¼ teaspoon cayenne pepper

Kosher salt and freshly ground black pepper

1 (28-ounce) can diced tomatoes

1 (16-ounce) can kidney beans, drained and rinsed

1 (16-ounce) can pinto beans, drained and rinsed

1 (15-ounce) can tomato juice

1 (15-ounce) can tomato sauce

Shredded cheese and crackers, for serving

DIRECTIONS

1. In a large skillet, combine the ground beef, onion, bell pepper, and garlic and cook over medium-high heat until the meat is no longer pink. Drain any excess fat from the skillet.

2. Transfer the mixture to a 6-quart slow cooker and add the chili powder, cumin, oregano, cayenne pepper, salt, and black pepper. Stir to combine.

3. Add the diced tomatoes, kidney beans, pinto beans, tomato juice, and tomato sauce to the slow cooker. Stir to combine. Cover and cook on Low for 7 to 8 hours.

4. Ladle into bowls and serve warm, topped with cheese and crackers.

Cincinnati Chili

Yield: Serves 6–8 | Prep Time: 10 minutes | Cook Time: 3 hours

While Cincinnati Chili could be eaten on its own, its true shining moment is when it's served over baked potatoes or pasta. That's how it was first served in the 1920s when it was developed by Greek-Macedonian restaurateurs. The combination of the spiciness of the chili powder mixed with the sweetness of the cinnamon makes this a dish you'll remember.

INGREDIENTS

2 pounds lean ground beef

1 onion, finely diced, plus more for serving

1 (15-ounce) can tomato sauce

3 garlic cloves, finely minced

1 teaspoon ground allspice

1 teaspoon ground cumin

3 tablespoons chili powder

1½ teaspoons ground cinnamon

1 tablespoon unsweetened cocoa powder

2 bay leaves

2 tablespoons apple cider vinegar

Kosher salt

Hot sauce, for serving

Cooked pasta of your choice, for serving

Shredded cheddar cheese, for serving

DIRECTIONS

1. In a large pot, combine the ground beef and 4 cups water. Bring to a boil over high heat, stirring the beef until it's well broken up. Reduce the heat to low and bring to a simmer. Cook for about 30 minutes, occasionally skimming off any fat and impurities that rise to the top.

2. Once the beef is cooked through, add the onion, tomato sauce, garlic, allspice, cumin, chili powder, cinnamon, cocoa powder, bay leaves, and vinegar. Stir to combine and increase the heat to medium-high. Bring to a boil, then reduce the heat to low and simmer once again, uncovered, for about 2½ hours. The chili will thicken as it cooks.

3. Remove from the heat and taste. Add salt if needed and add hot sauce, if desired.

4. Serve over cooked pasta and top with plenty of shredded cheese and diced onions.

Slow Cooker Chicken Enchilada Chili

Yield: Serves 6 | Prep Time: 10 minutes | Cook Time: 4 hours on High or 6 hours on Low

One night after cooking a batch of chili, I realized that I had used many of the same ingredients that I had to make chicken enchiladas the night before. From the onion to the bell pepper to the beans and the myriad of spices, this seemed like a mash-up just waiting to happen.

INGREDIENTS

1 (10-ounce) can red enchilada sauce

1 (14.5-ounce) can RoTel diced tomatoes with green chiles

1 (15-ounce) can chili beans in mild chili sauce

1 (15-ounce) can black beans, drained and rinsed

1½ cups frozen corn kernels

½ red bell pepper, seeded and diced

½ green bell pepper, seeded and diced

½ cup diced onion

1 pound boneless, skinless chicken breasts, cubed

½ teaspoon ground cumin

¾ teaspoon paprika

1½ tablespoons chili powder

2 cups low-sodium chicken broth

1 (8-ounce) package cream cheese, at room temperature

Kosher salt and freshly ground black pepper

Fresh cilantro and lime wedges, for garnish

DIRECTIONS

1. In a 6-quart slow cooker, combine the enchilada sauce, tomatoes with chiles, chili beans, black beans, frozen corn, bell peppers, onion, and chicken. Sprinkle the cumin, paprika, and chili powder over everything. Stir to combine and add the broth.

2. Cover and cook on High for 4 hours or on Low for 6 hours.

3. Add the cream cheese, stir well, and cover. Let sit for a few minutes, then, using a large spoon, briskly stir the cream cheese to melt and combine. Season with salt and black pepper.

4. Cover and cook on High until the cream cheese has completely melted, about 10 minutes.

5. Ladle into bowls and garnish with fresh cilantro and lime wedges.

Pulled Pork Chili

Yield: Serves 4 | Prep Time: 5 minutes | Cook Time: 30 minutes

The smoky barbecue taste of the pulled pork and fire-roasted tomatoes makes this an ideal dish to make in the summer (or even just when you're craving that reminder of sunshine in the winter). Fresh bacon will add a smokier quality, but you can substitute bacon bits if you wish.

INGREDIENTS

1 teaspoon olive oil

2 bacon slices, chopped

½ large onion, diced

2 (14.4-ounce) cans fire-roasted diced tomatoes

1 (16-ounce) can black beans, drained and rinsed

1 (16-ounce) can chili beans in sauce, undrained

1 (14.5-ounce) can chicken broth

1 pound prepared pulled pork (see Note)

DIRECTIONS

1. In a large pot, combine the olive oil and chopped bacon and cook over medium heat until the bacon is crisp, about 4 minutes. Transfer the bacon to a plate and set aside. Put the onion in the pot and cook, stirring, until the onion is softened, about 5 minutes.

2. Add the tomatoes, black beans, chili beans, and broth. Bring to a simmer and cook for 15 minutes.

3. Add the pulled pork and simmer for 5 minutes more. Stir in the bacon.

4. Ladle into bowls and serve.

NOTE

We used premade barbecued pork from the grocery store. You can find some in the deli aisle.

Slow Cooker Buffalo Chicken Chili

Yield: Serves 6–8 | Prep Time: 10 minutes | Cook Time: 3 hours on High or 6–8 hours on Low

You can build your preferred spice level in chili in a few different ways. You can mix in jalapeños, add various spices like red pepper flakes and chili seasoning, or incorporate different sauces, like Buffalo wing sauce. Pack up a thermos or two full of this and bring it with you when you go tailgating!

INGREDIENTS

1 pound boneless, skinless chicken thighs, cubed

1 (15.5-ounce) can cannellini beans, drained and rinsed

1 (14.5-ounce) can fire-roasted diced tomatoes, drained

4 cups chicken broth

½ cup buffalo wing sauce

1 (1-ounce) package dry ranch dressing mix

1 cup frozen corn kernels

2 garlic cloves, minced

½ cup chopped onion

Kosher salt and freshly ground black pepper

1 (8-ounce) package cream cheese, at room temperature

Blue cheese crumbles, for garnish

DIRECTIONS

1. In a sauté pan, quickly brown the chicken on all sides. The chicken will not be fully cooked through.

2. Transfer the chicken to a 6-quart slow cooker and add the beans, tomatoes, broth, wing sauce, ranch dressing mix, corn, garlic, and onion. Season with salt and pepper. Stir to combine.

3. Place the block of cream cheese on top of everything and cover. Cook on High for 3 hours or on Low for 6 hours, stirring occasionally to combine the cheese into the soup.

4. Ladle into bowls and serve topped with blue cheese crumbles.

Pale Ale Chili

Yield: Serves 6–8 | Prep Time: 10 minutes | Cook Time: 1½ hours

The pale ale adds a unique twist to this chili recipe. The bitterness of the hops enhances the flavor of the peppers while adding a distinct bite to the dish. The more bitter the beer, the spicier the dish will become, since the hops enhance the flavor of the peppers, so keep that in mind when choosing your pale ale.

INGREDIENTS

1 tablespoon olive oil

2 pounds beef stew meat

1 red bell pepper, seeded and diced

1 poblano pepper, seeded and diced

1 onion, diced

3 tablespoons chili powder

1 tablespoon ground cumin

2 teaspoons smoked paprika

1 (12-ounce) can pale ale

1 (14-ounce) can fire-roasted diced tomatoes

1 (15-ounce) can tomato sauce

Kosher salt and freshly ground black pepper

Sour cream, for garnish

DIRECTIONS

1. In a large pot, heat the olive oil over high heat. Working in batches, quickly brown the stew meat, transferring each batch to a bowl. Once all the meat is browned, set the bowl aside.

2. Add the bell pepper, poblano, and onion to the pot and cook for 5 minutes, until the vegetables are softened.

3. Return the meat to the pot, along with any juices from the bowl, and add the chili powder, cumin, paprika, pale ale, tomatoes, tomato sauce, salt, and black pepper.

4. Bring to a boil, then reduce the heat to low and simmer, covered, for at least 1 hour. The longer you cook the chili, the more tender the meat will be.

5. Ladle into bowls, top with sour cream, and serve.

7

Chowders and Bisques

What's the difference between soup and chowder? Chowders are soups that tend to have a cream or milk base and use flour as a thickening agent. My Midwest roots tend to lead me toward classics like the Midwest Corn Chowder (page 200), but I must say, I was digging the Southern vibes from the Sausage and Grits Chowder (page 212). Just as with soups, you have the option of sticking with tried-and-true favorites or experimenting and finding a new top pick.

Fisherman's Wharf Clam Chowder

Yield: Serves 4 | Prep Time: 5 minutes | Cook Time: 30 minutes

The first time I visited Boston, I headed down to the docks where I heard all the best seafood restaurants were. My friend and I ate lobster rolls and clam chowder on a beautiful, sunny summer day, and I immediately wanted to recreate that seafood feast at home. The delicate, mild flavor of this dish makes it the ideal dish for either lunch or a light dinner.

INGREDIENTS

1 tablespoon unsalted butter

1 small onion, chopped

1 celery stalk, chopped

4 small Yukon Gold potatoes, diced

2 tablespoons all-purpose flour

2 (6.5-ounce) cans chopped clams, undrained

1 cup seafood stock

2 cups chicken broth

½ teaspoon fresh thyme leaves

Kosher salt and freshly ground black pepper

2 cups heavy cream

Oyster crackers, for garnish

DIRECTIONS

1. In a large pot, melt the butter over medium heat. Add the onion, celery, and potatoes. Cook, stirring, for 3 to 5 minutes, or until the onion is translucent.

2. Sprinkle the mixture with the flour and stir until all the flour has been absorbed. Cook for 3 minutes more, until the mixture is a very pale brown.

3. Add the clams, seafood stock, broth, thyme, salt, and pepper; cover and bring to a boil.

4. Reduce the heat to low, and cook, covered, for 12 to 15 minutes, or until the potatoes are tender. Remove from the heat and stir in the cream. Return the pot to the heat and cook, stirring frequently, for 5 minutes, or until thickened.

5. Ladle into bowls, garnish with oyster crackers, and serve.

Midwest Corn Chowder

Yield: Serves 4–6 | Prep Time: 5 minutes | Cook Time: 30 minutes

Corn chowder was one of the first soups I ever made, and this classic version never gets old. The onion and potato give it a more dynamic flavor, while the bacon adds a crispiness that my husband and I love.

INGREDIENTS

5 bacon slices, chopped

1 cup chopped onion

5 red potatoes, cubed

1 bay leaf

1 (14.75-ounce) can cream-style corn

1 cup frozen corn kernels

1 cup whole milk

2 cups heavy cream

Kosher salt and freshly ground black pepper

DIRECTIONS

1. In a large pot, cook the bacon over medium-high heat until crisp. Transfer to a paper towel–lined plate and set aside.

2. Reduce the heat to medium, add the onion, and cook for 3 to 4 minutes, or until tender. Add the potatoes, bay leaf, and 1 cup water; bring to a boil. Reduce the heat to low and cover. Simmer for 18 to 20 minutes, or until the potatoes are tender.

3. Stir in the cream-style corn, frozen corn, milk, and heavy cream; cook, stirring often, for 5 minutes more, until the soup begins to simmer again. Remove the bay leaf. Taste and season with salt and pepper.

4. Ladle into bowls, sprinkle with the bacon, and serve immediately.

Potato-Ham Chowder

Yield: Serves 6 | Prep Time: 10 minutes | Cook Time: 1 hour

Nothing beats a pub atmosphere with the dimmed lighting, rowdy chatter, and relaxed vibe. The food itself can't be beat, either. It's a bit indulgent and greasy but always completely satisfying. I sought to create a chowder that would be worthy of making its way onto a pub menu. The chopped bacon on top adds a nice crunch that pairs nicely against the creaminess of the broth, creating the cozy, comforting dish I wanted.

INGREDIENTS

4 tablespoons (½ stick) unsalted butter

1 onion, diced

2 celery stalks, chopped

2 garlic cloves, minced

4–5 Yukon Gold potatoes, diced

1½ cups frozen corn kernels

1 (8-ounce) ham steak, cubed

2 teaspoons fresh thyme leaves

Kosher salt and freshly ground black pepper

2 tablespoons all-purpose flour

2 cups vegetable broth

3½ cups whole milk

Chopped scallions, for garnish

Cooked bacon, crumbled, for garnish

DIRECTIONS

1. In a large pot, melt the butter over medium heat. Stir in the onion and celery and cook until the onion is translucent and the celery begins to soften. Add the garlic, stir, and cook until fragrant.

2. Add the potatoes, corn, ham, and thyme to the pot. Season with salt and pepper. Stir in the flour and cook for 1 to 2 minutes. Add the broth and bring to a boil. Reduce the heat to low and simmer gently, until the potatoes are tender, about 45 minutes.

3. Remove from the heat and stir in the milk. Cook until the soup begins to bubble again.

4. Ladle into bowls, garnish with scallions and bacon, and serve.

Corn-Zucchini Chowder

Yield: Serves 4–6 | Prep Time: 5 minutes | Cook Time: 30 minutes

While the corn and the zucchini are the two stars of this chowder, the addition of onion, bell pepper, and potatoes make this a vegetable cornucopia! I get a new burst of flavor in each spoonful in a comforting, creamy broth, making it a hit every summer.

INGREDIENTS

2 tablespoons unsalted butter

1 cup chopped onion

1 red bell pepper, diced

4 Yukon Gold potatoes, cubed

1 bay leaf

1 (14.75-ounce) can cream-style corn

1 cup frozen corn kernels

1 zucchini, diced

1 cup whole milk

2 cups heavy cream

Kosher salt and freshly ground black pepper

DIRECTIONS

1. In a large pot, melt the butter over medium-high heat. Add the onion and bell pepper. Cook for 3 to 4 minutes, or until tender. Add the potatoes, bay leaf, and 1 cup water; bring to a boil. Reduce the heat to low and cover. Simmer for 18 to 20 minutes, or until the potatoes are tender.

2. Stir in the cream-style corn, frozen corn, zucchini, milk, and heavy cream. Cook, stirring often, for 5 minutes, until the soup begins to simmer again. Remove the bay leaf. Taste and season with salt and black pepper.

3. Ladle into bowls and serve immediately.

Roasted Cauliflower Chowder

Yield: Serves 4–6 | Prep Time: 10 minutes | Cook Time: 45 minutes

This chowder is so reliable because it's easily adjustable to different dietary restrictions. If you omit the shredded cheese garnish, it's a completely vegan recipe (thanks to the use of creamy almond milk!), and if you'd like, you can use gluten-free flour instead of all-purpose flour and eliminate the crackers to make it a completely gluten-free recipe, too.

INGREDIENTS

1 head cauliflower, coarsely chopped

1 head garlic, top cut off

1 large shallot, coarsely chopped

2 tablespoons olive oil

Kosher salt and freshly ground black pepper

2 carrots, chopped

2 celery stalks, chopped

1 bay leaf

1 teaspoon fresh thyme leaves

¼ cup all-purpose flour

2 (15-ounce) cans vegetable broth

2 cups unsweetened almond milk

¼ cup shredded white cheddar cheese, for garnish (optional)

Saltine crackers, for garnish

DIRECTIONS

1. Preheat the oven to 400°F.

2. Place the cauliflower, garlic, and shallot on a large baking sheet. Drizzle with 1 tablespoon of the olive oil, sprinkle with salt and pepper, and toss until well coated. Roast for 20 to 25 minutes, or until the cauliflower is lightly browned and tender. Remove from the oven and set aside.

3. In a large pot, heat the remaining 1 tablespoon olive oil over medium heat. Add the carrots and celery and cook, stirring occasionally, for 5 minutes.

4. Squeeze the roasted garlic from the papery skins and finely chop. Add the garlic, roasted cauliflower, roasted shallot, bay leaf, and thyme to the pot. Sprinkle the flour over everything and stir. Cook until all the flour has been absorbed, about 5 minutes.

5. Stir in the broth. Simmer for 10 minutes. Add the milk and stir until the chowder is creamy. Season with salt and pepper.

6. Ladle the chowder into bowls and serve warm, topped with shredded cheese, if desired, and crackers.

Bayou Crab Chowder

Yield: Serves 4–6 | Prep Time: 10 minutes | Cook Time: 20 minutes

A little bit smoky and a little bit spicy, this crab chowder is a true Cajun delight. I've used a few shortcuts with the addition of refrigerated potatoes, frozen corn, and canned crabmeat, which is perfect for making this year-round.

INGREDIENTS

6 bacon slices

12 ounces refrigerated diced potatoes

7 ounces turkey kielbasa, chopped

1½ cups frozen corn kernels

4 cups vegetable broth

2 garlic cloves, minced

1 tablespoon Cajun seasoning, plus more for garnish

2 sprigs fresh thyme

Kosher salt and freshly ground black pepper

2 cups half-and-half

2 (8-ounce) cans crabmeat

DIRECTIONS

1. Heat a large pot over medium-high heat. Add the bacon and cook until crisp. Transfer the bacon to a paper towel–lined plate and set aside.

2. Add the potatoes, kielbasa, corn, broth, garlic, Cajun seasoning, thyme, salt, and pepper to the pot and bring to a boil. Cover and reduce the heat to low. Simmer until the potatoes are heated through, about 5 minutes.

3. Stir in the half-and-half and all but ½ cup of the crabmeat. Remove the thyme stems and remove the pot from the heat.

4. Ladle into bowls and garnish with the remaining crabmeat and a sprinkle of Cajun seasoning.

Cheesy Italian Sausage Chowder

Yield: Serves 6 | Prep Time: 10 minutes | Cook Time: 20 minutes

This is the ultimate chowder for those crisper-than-usual days before winter hits. It has the makings of a true country-style feast, including potatoes, cream, hearty sausage, and, of course, plenty of cheese.

INGREDIENTS

1 pound hot or mild bulk Italian sausage

½ onion, diced

2 celery stalks, chopped

1 tablespoon all-purpose flour

Freshly ground black pepper

4–5 Yukon Gold potatoes, diced

3 cups low-sodium chicken broth

1 cup heavy cream

1 cup shredded cheddar cheese, plus more for garnish

Scallions, thinly sliced, for garnish

DIRECTIONS

1. In a large pot, brown the sausage, onion, and celery over medium-high heat. Drain the excess fat and sprinkle with the flour and plenty of pepper. Stir well and cook until all the flour has been absorbed, about 3 minutes.

2. Stir in the potatoes and broth. Bring to a gentle boil, then reduce the heat to low. Cover and simmer for 15 minutes, or until the potatoes are tender. Stir in the cream and cheddar cheese. Remove from the heat once all the cheese has melted.

3. Ladle into large bowls. Serve topped with additional cheese and scallions.

Sausage and Grits Chowder

Yield: Serves 6–8 | Prep Time: 10 minutes | Cook Time: 20 minutes

I grew up in Minnesota, so it took until after I graduated high school to even try grits for the first time! Grits are made from corn that's been ground until coarse and then boiled. It has a similar consistency to porridge or polenta. In this recipe, the grits add a rich, thick texture that makes this a superb stand-alone dish.

INGREDIENTS

1 pound bulk turkey sausage

2 tablespoons all-purpose flour

Freshly ground black pepper

1 (15-ounce) can creamed corn

2–3 Yukon Gold potatoes, diced

3 cups whole milk

1 (15-ounce) can low-sodium chicken broth

1 tablespoon Cajun seasoning

3 cups quick grits

½ cup shredded white cheddar cheese

DIRECTIONS

1. In a large pot, brown the sausage over medium-high heat. Drain the excess fat and sprinkle with flour and plenty of pepper. Stir well and cook until all the flour has been absorbed, about 3 minutes.

2. Stir in the creamed corn, potatoes, milk, broth, and Cajun seasoning. Bring to a gentle boil, then reduce the heat to low. Cover and simmer for 15 minutes, or until the potatoes are tender.

3. Just before serving, prepare the grits according to the package directions. Stir in the cheddar cheese until melted.

4. Ladle the sausage chowder into bowls and top with a generous scoop of grits. Serve.

Bacon Cheeseburger Chowder

Yield: Serves 6–8 | Prep Time: 10 minutes | Cook Time: 30 minutes

For the most part, I try to eat relatively healthy. When chowders like this enter my life, however, I can't help but indulge a little. It has everything you could ask for from a soup: lots of cheese, beef, potatoes, and, best of all, lots of bacon.

INGREDIENTS

1 pound lean ground beef

1 onion, diced

2 celery stalks, chopped

1 red bell pepper, diced

2 garlic cloves, minced

2 tablespoons all-purpose flour

2 cups whole milk

1 pound small red potatoes, quartered

1 cup beef broth

12 ounces Velveeta cheese, cut into small pieces

8 bacon slices, cooked and crumbled, for garnish

2 hamburger buns, toasted and torn in pieces, for garnish

DIRECTIONS

1. In a large pot, put in the beef, onion, celery, and pepper over medium heat. Cook for 8 minutes, until the meat is cooked through completely. Carefully drain off any fat. Add the garlic and cook for 1 minute.

2. Stir in the flour and cook until all the flour has been absorbed. Stir in the milk, potatoes, and broth. Bring to a boil, reduce the heat to low, and cover. Simmer for 20 minutes, or until the potatoes are tender.

3. Add the cheese and stir until it has melted and the soup is well combined.

4. Ladle into bowls and top each with crumbled bacon and toasted bun pieces. Serve.

Asiago Bisque

Yield: Serves 6–8 | Prep Time: 20 minutes | Cook Time: 40 minutes

I grew up one state away from the cheese capital of America: Wisconsin. When my family and I went on road trips down to Wisconsin, we'd stop at the first cheese store we found and stock up on different cheeses. Asiago cheese was near the top of my list, and it works beautifully in this soup, giving it a sweet, nutty flavor.

INGREDIENTS

10 tablespoons (1¼ sticks) unsalted butter

1 cup chopped shallots

1 cup chopped onions

1½ cups chopped carrots

1 cup chopped celery

3 cups chopped, peeled potatoes, cut into bite-size chunks

2 cups chicken broth

1 cup white wine

1 tablespoon finely chopped fresh rosemary, plus more leaves for garnish

2 cups heavy cream

2 cups shredded Asiago cheese, plus more for serving

1 head roasted garlic (see Note)

Kosher salt and freshly ground black pepper

6 bacon slices, cooked and crumbled, for garnish

DIRECTIONS

1. In a large saucepan, melt the butter over medium heat. Add the shallots, onions, carrots, and celery and cook until tender, about 6 minutes.

2. Add the potatoes, broth, wine, and rosemary. Cover and cook for 20 minutes.

3. Add the cream and cook for 5 minutes more.

4. Remove the pan from the heat and stir in the Asiago until melted.

5. Carefully transfer the soup to a blender, add the roasted garlic, and puree until smooth and creamy. (Alternatively, blend the soup directly in the pot using an immersion blender.) Season with salt and pepper.

6. Ladle into bowls and serve topped with more Asiago, the bacon, and rosemary.

NOTE

To make roasted garlic, cut the top third from 1 head garlic to expose the cloves. Drizzle with some olive oil, wrap in foil, and roast in a 400°F oven for 45 minutes. Squeeze the cloves from the papery skins.

Easy Lobster Bisque

Yield: Serves 6 | Prep Time: 10 minutes | Cook Time: 1 hour

The lobster in this recipe maintains its firm texture and sweet yet mild flavor, all while bathed in a creamy milk broth. I recommend using a dry white wine like Pinot Grigio or Sauvignon Blanc to help enhance the flavors of the dish.

INGREDIENTS

2 cups water

4 lobster tails, about 4 ounces each

1 tablespoon kosher salt

2 tablespoons olive oil

1 onion, finely diced

1 fennel bulb, thinly sliced, fronds reserved for garnish

2 garlic cloves, minced

2 tablespoons tomato paste

2 cups white wine

3 sprigs fresh thyme

1 bay leaf

½ teaspoon cayenne pepper

2 cups low-sodium chicken broth

2 cups seafood stock

1 (15-ounce) can diced tomatoes

½ cup heavy cream

½ cup half-and-half

1 lemon, halved

DIRECTIONS

1. In a large pot, bring 2 cups water to a simmer. Add the lobster tails and salt. Cover and simmer for about 8 minutes, or until the tails are cooked through. Transfer the tails to a plate and let cool. Once cool, remove the meat from the shells, coarsely chop, and set aside. Reserve the shells.

2. In a large pot, heat the olive oil over medium-high heat. Add the onion and fennel. Cook until the onion is translucent and the fennel is softened. Stir in the garlic and tomato paste. Cook for 2 to 3 minutes more, until the mixture begins to turn a deep red color.

3. Add the wine to the pot, being sure to scrape up the flavorful bits from the bottom of the pan. Add the thyme, bay leaf, and cayenne. Cook for 2 minutes, then add the broth, seafood stock, reserved lobster shells, and tomatoes. Bring the soup to a simmer and cook for 50 minutes.

4. Carefully remove the thyme stems, bay leaf, and lobster shells from the pot. Using an immersion blender, blend directly in the pot until smooth. Stir in the cream and half-and-half.

5. Divide the lobster meat among six soup bowls and ladle the soup over the top. Squeeze lemon juice over the top and garnish with fennel fronds. Serve.

Cajun Shrimp Bisque

Yield: Serves 4 | Prep Time: 30 minutes | Cook Time: 15 minutes

Shrimp is a staple ingredient in a traditional Cajun feast. When I went to visit a friend in New Orleans, we wound up eating seafood every single night I was there. The whole milk in this recipe makes this bisque extra thick and creamy.

INGREDIENTS

Shrimp Stock

6 cups water

1 pound raw shrimp, peeled and deveined, shells reserved

½ onion, quartered

1 teaspoon kosher salt

2 bay leaves

Bisque

4 tablespoons (½ stick) unsalted butter

½ onion, finely diced

2 celery stalks, finely diced

3 garlic cloves, minced

2 tablespoons all-purpose flour

2 tablespoons concentrated tomato paste

3 cups whole milk

1 bay leaf

4 fresh basil leaves, chopped

3 tablespoons hot sauce

Kosher salt and freshly ground black pepper

Oyster crackers, for serving

DIRECTIONS

1. *For the shrimp stock:* Bring the water to a boil in a large pot. Add the shrimp shells (reserve the shrimp meat for the bisque), onion, salt, and bay leaves. Boil gently for 30 minutes. Remove from the heat and carefully strain the stock into a container; discard the solids.

2. *For the bisque:* In a large skillet, melt the butter over medium-high heat. Add the onion, celery, and garlic. Cook, stirring, until soft, about 5 minutes. Add the flour and tomato paste and toss to coat the veggies. Cook for 2 minutes, until all the flour has been absorbed. Remove the pan from the heat.

3. Stir in the shrimp stock and whisk until combined and there are no lumps. Stir in the milk. Add the bay leaf, basil, and hot sauce. Put back on the heat and bring to a boil; reduce the heat to low and simmer for 10 minutes. Taste and season with salt and pepper.

4. Add the reserved shrimp and simmer until the shrimp are cooked through, about 2 minutes.

5. Remove from the heat, remove the bay leaf, ladle into bowls, and serve with oyster crackers.

Acknowledgments

Thank you to my incredible culinary and creative team at Prime Publishing. Megan Von Schönhoff and Tom Krawczyk, my photographers. Chris Hammond and Marlene Stolfo, my culinary test kitchen geniuses. To word masters and editors Bryn Clark and Jessica Thelander. And to my amazing editor and friend, Kara Rota. Thank you to Stuart Hochwert and the entire Prime Publishing team for their enthusiasm and support. Thank you to Will Schwalbe, Erica Martirano, Justine Sha, Brant Janeway, Jaclyn Waggner, and the entire staff at St. Martin's Griffin for helping this book come to life. This book was a team effort, filled with collaboration and creativity that reached no limits.

Index

About the Author

After receiving her master's in culinary arts at Auguste Escoffier in Avignon, France, Addie stayed in France to learn from Christian Etienne at his three-Michelin-star restaurant. Upon leaving France, she spent the next several years working with restaurant groups. She worked in the kitchen for Daniel Boulud and moved coast to coast with Thomas Keller, building a career in management, restaurant openings, and brand development. She later joined Martha Stewart Living Omnimedia, where she worked with the editorial team as well as in marketing and sales. While living in New York, Addie completed her bachelor's degree in organizational behavior. Upon leaving New York, Addie joined gravitytank, an innovation consultancy in Chicago. As a culinary designer at gravitytank, Addie designed new food products for companies large and small. She created edible prototypes for clients and research participants to taste and experience, some of which you may see in stores today. In 2015, she debuted on the Food Network, where she competed on *Cutthroat Kitchen*, and won! And in 2017, she was a contestant on season 13 of *Food Network Star*.

Addie is the executive producer for RecipeLion. She oversees and creates culinary content for multiple web platforms and communities, leads video strategy, and oversees the production of in-print books. Addie is passionate about taking easy recipes and making them elegant, without making them complicated. From fine dining to entertaining, to innovation and test kitchens, Addie's experience with food makes these recipes unique and delicious.

Addie and her husband live in Lake Forest, Illinois, with their baby boy and happy puppy, Paisley. Addie is actively involved with youth culinary programs in the Chicagoland area, serving on the board of a bakery and catering company that employs at-risk youth. She is a healthy-foods teacher for first-graders in a low-income school district, and aside from eating and entertaining with friends and family, she loves encouraging kids to be creative in the kitchen!